VW Beetle
The Complete Story

Other Titles in the Crowood AutoClassic Series

VW BEETLE
The Complete Story

Robert Davies

First published in 1996 by
The Crowood Press Ltd
Ramsbury, Marlborough
Wiltshire SN8 2HR

British Library Cataloguing-in-Publication Data

A catalogue record for this book is available from the British
Library.

ISBN 1 85223 953 0

Dedication

For Jo

Picture Credits

All black and white photographs supplied by AutoMuseum Volkswagen. *VW Motoring,
Popular Classics*, Graham Robson and The National Motor Museum, Beaulieu
All colour photography by the author

Printed and bound in Great Britain by BPC Books Ltd, Aylesbury

Contents

Acknowledgements

My heartfelt thanks go to all those who have helped me in gathering the vast and varied amount of material that has gone into this book. Among those who deserve a particular mention are: VAG (UK), AutoMuseum Volkswagen, VW de Mexico, VW do Brasil, *VW Motoring*, *Popular Classics*, URO Automotive, Kevin Eade (Surrey Air-Cooled Owners Club), John Daniel (London & Thames Valley VWOC), Howard Cheese (Mexican Brazilian Beetle Register), Dr Rod Oakland (The Psywar Society), Graham Robson and, last but not least, Simon and Tracy Hall.

For providing their cars for the colour photography in this book, a special thank you goes to the following owners: Peter Colborne-Baber (1947 1200), Arthur Carr (1956 1200), Shane Covey (1970 1300), William Von Siegmund (1979 Cabriolet), and Martin Butler (1985 Jubilee).

Preface

What was the most significant car of the twentieth century? It's an obvious question, and there are plenty of obvious candidates to choose from. None merits the accolade more than the Volkswagen Beetle.

The Beetle wins firstly through sheer weight of numbers. More than 21 million have been built over seven decades of production, which makes it decisively the most numerous car of the century.

But the Beetle's claim goes deeper than simple numbers. No other model illustrates so thoroughly twentieth century society's deep and multi-faceted fascination with the motor car.

At face value, the Beetle is just a means of transport – and a superbly effective one at that. Beetles have taken cheap, reliable and economical motoring all over the world to both affluent and developing countries alike. But wherever the Beetle has sold, it has come to mean more than just a method of getting from A to B.

From Brazilian doctor to German farmhand, Australian student to Californian surfer, people have fallen in love with the Beetle, and their enthusiasm for their cars has become legendary.

The Beetle's own story is the stuff of legend too. It was conceived in Germany in the 1930s as the idealistic vision of an inspired engineer who wanted everybody to enjoy a freedom of movement unknown to previous generations.

With a little help from a mad dictator, he brought the Beetle to life. War threatened to smother it at birth, but a far-sighted British soldier resurrected it from the ashes of war-torn Germany. A single-minded businessman then took it on to phenomenal sales success, breaking every motor industry rule in the process.

Today, the Beetle continues to break all the rules. It's still in production in Mexico and Brazil, decades after its contemporaries were consigned to the scrapheap. Everywhere else, enthusiasts of all hues, backgrounds and ages labour to keep their cherished classic Beetles on the road.

They know that of all the creations of the twentieth century, the VW Beetle is a very special one.

A Brief History of the Beetle

1932	Ferdinand Porsche designs the Type 12, his first 'people's car' with Beetle characteristics.
1933	The Porsche Type 32 prototype is designed for NSU. It looks still more Beetle-like, with torsion bar suspension and a rear-mounted air-cooled engine.
1934	Ferdinand Porsche presents his proposals for a people's car (Volkswagen) to the German government, and is commissioned to make prototypes.
1935	The first Beetle prototypes, the V1 saloon and V2 cabriolet, are built.
1936	Three further prototypes, the VW3 series, are made.
1937	Another thirty prototypes (VW30), looking increasingly Beetle-like, are put through a rigorous long-distance testing procedure.
1938	Production details are finalised in a new batch of prototypes (VW38). Adolf Hitler gives them the name KdF-Wagen at the inauguration of the VW factory at Wolfsburg.
1939 – 1944	Wartime production at Wolfsburg switches to military VWs, the Kübelwagen and its derivatives. Bombing raids late in the war leave the factory partially destroyed.
1945	VW factory comes under the control of the British Army. Limited production of the Beetle begins.
1946	Beetle production reaches 10,000.
1947	VW Beetle is officially launched, fitted with a 1,131cc 25bhp engine. First exports begin to Holland; in the UK, John Colborne-Baber starts offering rhd conversions on privately imported cars.
1948	Heinrich Nordhoff takes over as Director-General of VW.
1949	Export/DeLuxe model is launched with improved trim. VW establishes an import agency in the US. Cabriolets by Karmann and Hebmüller go on sale.
1950	Beetle gains hydraulic brakes and improved ventilation. The practical Type 2 Beetle-derived Transporter is launched.
1952	Hebmüller is declared bankrupt, having produced just 750 Cabriolets. The first factory-built rhd Beetle arrives in the UK. Gearbox now has synchromesh on second, third and fourth gears.
1953	Oval rear window replaces traditional split screen. From December engine capacity increases to 1,192cc (30bhp).
1955	Launch of the VW Karmann-Ghia coupé, based on Beetle running gear. Over a million Beetles have now been built. VW adopts an August-to-August production year.
1957	Karmann-Ghia convertible launched. Beetle receives a facelift, with enlarged glass area and a rectangular rear screen, and a new dashboard.
1960	Engine revised to give 34bhp. All-synchro gearbox, automatic choke and flashing indicators fitted.

1961	Fuel gauge fitted and reserve tap deleted; worm and peg steering replaced by worm and roller; front luggage capacity enlarged.
1964	Glass area enlarged and a slightly curved windscreen fitted.
1965	Beetle 1300 launched, with 1285cc 40bhp engine and ventilated wheels; maintenance-free balljoints replace kingpins on front suspension. Annual Beetle production now exceeds one million.
1966	Beetle 1500 launched, with 1493cc 44bhp engine and front disc brakes. Rear track is widened and equaliser spring introduced to reduce oversteer.
1967	Major facelift gives Beetle upright headlamps and raised bumpers. Dual-circuit brakes and 12-volt electrics arrive. Beetle 1500 Automatic is launched with three-speed semi-automatic transmission and double-jointed rear suspension. Total Beetle production has now passed 10 million.
1968	Heinrich Nordhof dies aged 69. Semi-auto option is extended to 1300.
1970	Launch of the Super Beetles: 1285cc (44bhp) 1302 and 1584cc (50bhp) 1302S. These have a restyled front end with MacPherson strut front suspension and extra boot space, plus double-jointed rear suspension and twin inlet-port engines. Beetle 1500 is dropped.
1972	Super Beetles are rebadged 1303 and 1303S, and have bigger 'panoramic' wind screens, large rear lamp clusters, and a redesigned black plastic dashboard. Beetle passes the production record of 15,007,033 set by the Ford Model T.
1974	Beetle production at Wolfsburg ceases in July, but continues in Germany at Emden. Super Beetles get rack and pinion steering.
1975	Production of Super Beetles ceases (but Cabriolet continues to be based on 1303S).
1978	The last German-built Beetle saloon leaves the Emden factory in January. European sales of imported Mexican 1200 saloons continue.
1980	Production of Cabriolet ceases in January.
1992	Mexico builds the 21 millionth Beetle.
1994	VW unveil Concept 1, a Beetle-style city car. Unexpected public demand causes VW to announce that a vehicle based on Concept 1 will go into production before the end of the century.
1996	Beetle production continues in Mexico and Brazil, more than 60 years after the first Beetle prototypes were designed. Concept 1 is named the New Beetle.

1 Evolution of a People's Car

It was, I believe, Edgar Wallace who suggested that if a person has one nickname he is held in some esteem, but if he has two or more he is disliked. Obviously the same can't be said about cars, for the Beetle – surely the most loved car of all time – has been given an affectionate nickname in just about every country where it has sold.

In America it's known as the 'Bug', in Germany, it's the 'Käfer', in France the 'Coccinelle', in Brazil the 'Fusca' and in Italy the 'Maggiolino'. Translated, most of these nicknames are a variation on the Beetle theme and, of course, they refer to the car's characteristic humpty-backed styling. Before it earned its nicknames, which, like 'Beetle' in Britain, often became so ingrained in common usage that they were even adopted by the local VW concessionaire, the Beetle was simply known as the Volkswagen. While the Beetle nickname neatly described what the car looked like, 'Volkswagen' described its purpose in life.

In English, Volkswagen means 'people's car'. It was intended to signify, in the era before mass car ownership, that this was a vehicle which could be owned by anyone, no matter what their class, status or wealth. It meant a no-frills, practical, small car sold at a price that anyone could afford. It offered an opportunity for the man in the street to become the man in a car on the street. Today, with the number of Beetles built exceeding 21.3 million and

still rising, this original objective has been emphatically achieved.

It's rather ironic, therefore, that the designer and visionary behind the Volkswagen, Ferdinand Porsche, should now be best known for the marque of

A stubborn, single-minded engineering genius, Ferdinand Porsche kept his dream of a practical, inexpensive people's car alive in the face of decades of opposition from the German motor industry.

exclusive high-performance cars that bear his name. In the aftermath of World War Two, Ferdinand's son, Ferry, capitalized on the family firm's links with Volkswagen to develop sports cars derived from the Beetle. The first was the Porsche 356, which shared the Beetle's engine and suspension. Its successor, the Porsche 911, was launched in 1964, and like the Beetle, the 911 has become the most successful and long-lived vehicle in its field. Although it has developed in a very different direction to the Beetle, a glance at even a contemporary Porsche 911 reveals just how strong the link between these two cars still is.

Like the Beetle, the 911 has a rear engine, pushing the car along instead of pulling it like almost every other modern front-engined design. Listen and you'll hear the familiar burble of an air-cooled boxer engine, though the 911 has two more cylinders than its cousin. The torsion bar suspension layout fitted to 911s right up till the end of the 1980s was also derived from that fitted to the Beetle. The 911 even echoes the Beetle's bulbous bodywork and cheeky grin. Both look, sound and perform like no other car – and both owe their existence to Ferdinand Porsche.

Since his earliest days in the fledgling

Ferdinand Porsche – father of the Beetle

One of the greatest engineers of the twentieth century, visionary and designer of the world's most successful car, Ferdinand Porsche started life in humble surroundings. He was born in 1875 in Maffersdorf, Austria, a sleepy village best known for its carpet-weaving tradition. Ferdinand was a quiet but imaginative child, more interested in concocting his own experiments than following formal school lessons. But as he grew older his remarkable aptitude for engineering began to emerge.

This didn't go down well with his father, a tinsmith who was determined his son should follow him into the family business. In those days the father was very much the head of the family, and for Porsche senior this matter wasn't up for discussion. Ferdinand used to retreat to the attic to carry out experiments. Once, his father stormed in, and in a rage trampled on the equipment set out on the floor. In the process Porsche senior knocked over a battery which spilled acid on his shoes, scorching them and giving him an even worse temper.

But Ferdinand had inherited his father's stubborn streak. His fascination with the new power source electricity brought the family disagreement to a head. Electricity had only recently arrived in the village, and when Ferdinand saw it being used in a local carpet shop he was fascinated. Taking advantage of his father's absence on a trip for a few days, he rigged up electric lights in the family home. For a fifteen-year-old with no special training, working in a new and unknown medium, this was a precocious achievement. When his father returned, Ferdinand lit the house during dinner. Even Porsche senior couldn't fail to be impressed and, begrudgingly, he gave his consent for Ferdinand to leave home to study at the Technical University in Vienna.

Porsche's interest in electricity got him his first job, with electrical company Bela Egger. It naturally followed that when he moved to Lohner and made his first contribution to motoring design, it would take the form of a vehicle driven by electric motors mounted in the wheel hubs. This design neatly did away with the need for chains or driveshafts to transmit the power from engine to wheels.

At this time – around the turn of the century – there was no automatic assumption that motor cars should be powered by the internal combustion engine. Steam was a popular alternative, but for many engineers, Porsche included, electricity looked like the logical power source. No one had coined the term 'environmentally-friendly' back then, but it didn't take an engineering genius to

appreciate how much smoother, quieter and cleaner an electrical engine was than one which relied on internal combustion. A hundred years on, of course, engineers are still struggling to make this 'ideal' medium practical as a means of propelling a car at sensible speeds over useful distances.

The Lohner-Porsche electric car was shown at the 1900 Paris exhibition, and as a demonstration, Porsche drove it from Paris to Versailles at an average speed of 20mph (30km/h). It attracted a great deal of attention and sold well – in 1901 the London Fire Brigade took up Porsche's hub drive system.

Later, Porsche designed a hybrid electric/petrol engine for the car, giving up to 80bhp, but Lohner was beginning to chafe at the expense of building the endless stream of prototypes that Porsche kept coming up with. He moved to Austro-Daimler and embarked on the career that led to his quest for a people's car, and his decisive meeting with Adolf Hitler which brought about the Beetle.

Hitler, like Porsche, was an Austrian by birth and they both spoke the same dialect. Each had a vision of a people's car, and Hitler, who greatly admired Porsche's engineering skills, invested a lot of faith in Porsche's ability to turn this vision into reality.

The backdrop to this was a German political scene that was turning increasingly fascist. In 1933, Hitler took power in a Germany still shaken by the aftermath of World War One. He pulled the country together again, reaffirming its national identity and uniting popular opinion in a fervour of aggressively nationalistic militarism – all, of course, at the expense of those who didn't fit into his grand scheme. Unions were disbanded and replaced by Hitler's tame German Workers Front (DAF), and the persecution of minority groups began.

Whatever political views Porsche had, he kept them to himself, for he had his own ambitions, and the Nazi regime gave him the chance to fulfil them. His son Ferry explains in his autobiography: 'My father was basically a completely apolitical person who at that time was enjoying opportunities for work that he had never imagined in his wildest dreams'.

In 1934 Hitler wrote to Porsche, inviting 'the greatest German motor engineer' to apply for German nationality. It was not an invitation Porsche could refuse, and he acquiesced without comment. In 1938 Porsche received from Hitler the German National Prize – Germany's equivalent of a Nobel Prize. But there's no evidence to suggest Porsche genuinely supported the Nazis. On the contrary, it's striking that in photographs taken at the official Nazi functions Porsche attended, he

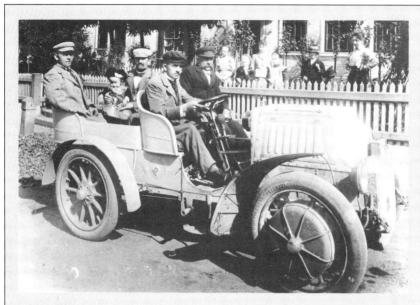

At the wheel of the 1902 Lohner-Porsche he designed, Ferdinand Porsche proudly takes his family for a spin. This model was powered by electric motors installed in the front wheel hubs.

is invariably seen wearing civilian clothes – often he cuts a conspicuous figure, clothed in the sole grey overcoat submerged in a sea of Nazi uniforms.

Porsche, we know, was notable for his stubbornness and determination. Sparing with praise, he had inherited his father's intolerance of contradictions and ruled his household in true patriarchal style. While working at Bela Egger, he had met and married his wife, Louise Kaes, and in 1909 she gave birth to their son Ferry, who would later build the family company into one of the world's most prestigious motor manufacturers.

Porsche's appetite for work left him little time or desire to relax. Unusually for the time, he had no passion for hunting – except, like many central Europeans, for mushrooms. He loved the cinema, and made the most of his trips to America to watch movies not permitted in Nazi Germany. But mostly he could be found in his cottage on the outskirts of Wolfsburg, discussing his latest engineering project over his favourite meal – Hungarian Goulash with lashings of paprika.

When war came Porsche continued to work at the Volkswagen factory, where production switched to military hardware. As well as vehicles based on the KdF-Wagen, Junkers bombers were built there, as were V1 flying bombs – the 'Doodlebugs' that fell in their thousands on London during the latter part of the war.

After the war Porsche was briefly detained by the occupying forces on suspicion of being a Nazi. But the former minister of munitions spoke up for him, saying that Porsche had simply been a designer who had no interest in politics. Released, Porsche returned briefly to Austria. Then, in November 1945, he was requested to travel to the French occupied zone. At this time there was still a possibility that Volkswagen production would be moved to France, and he responded with interest. But, instead, Porsche suddenly found himself accused of war crimes – using slave labour at the VW factory – and he was thrown into prison.

This time it took a lot longer to establish Porsche's innocence. He was taken to Paris, where he was obliged to work on the Renault 4CV – a concept not so far removed from his Volkswagen. The 4CV was in its final development, however, and Porsche suggested only minor modifications.

In September 1947 Porsche was released on bail of Fr500,000. This enormous sum, far more than Porsche could have found himself, was put forward by Piero Dusio, an Italian industrialist for whom the Porsche firm designed the Cisitalia T360 Grand Prix car. But it wasn't until 1949 that the French courts declared Porsche to be innocent and allowed him to return to Germany. By this time the great engineer was nearly seventy-five years old and his health was failing.

In his absence, son Ferry had been at work designing cars of his own, and the Porsche firm was brought back to life in October 1949. Ferdinand – who was presented with a black Porsche 356 on his seventy-fifth birthday – lived to see more than 400 cars bearing his name produced before he died of a stroke in January 1951. It is said, though, that what moved him to tears on his return to Germany was the sight of his Volkswagen travelling in droves along the autobahns.

After his wrongful arrest after the war, Porsche came home to find the 356, first in an illustrious series of sports cars bearing his name. But it was the Beetle in the background that probably brought him even more happiness.

motor industry during the first decade of this century, Porsche had nurtured a dream to build a cheap, small car that would make motoring accessible to the vast majority of people. It took thirty years and the intervention of fate in the form of an obsessive, power-crazed dictator to become reality.

There was a big problem that had first to be overcome, however. Porsche's ambition was, to his motor industry contemporaries, a disturbingly radical one. Across the Atlantic in America, where the Model T

Ford opened up personal transport to millions, a desire to build a car for the masses would have been regarded as acceptable, even admirable. But in Europe, the car was still regarded as a plaything for the rich, an expensive luxury which should be built with the same painstaking craftsmanship that had gone into the ornate horsedrawn carriages of the previous century.

This view suited the conservative car manufacturers, who saw no reason to abandon the lucrative business of making a

Ferdinand Porsche stands alongside a 1929 Steyr XXX. This was the sort of luxury car he was continually asked to design, when all the time he was itching to build something smaller, simpler and cheaper.

Porsche's passion for motor racing was an important influence on his car designs. Here he's piloting the 1910 Prinz Heinrich racer – its Tulpenwagen *(Tulip car) nickname reflected Porche's efforts to streamline its bodywork.*

few cars with high profit margins and start to experiment in the risky territory of mass production. Porsche's ambition, therefore, met stubborn opposition wherever he tried to realize it.

Porsche had enough ability to excel in his chosen profession despite this. In particular, his interest in racing led him to design a number of successful competition cars. Determined and hard-working, Porsche rapidly developed his career, and by 1916 he had established himself as managing director of Austro-Daimler. Here his dream of a people's car brought him into conflict – a theme that was to recur again and again in his working life. His efforts to divert Austro-Daimler, known for producing large luxury cars, into building smaller, less expensive, cars caused increasing tensions in the board room. In 1923 this culminated in an almighty row, and Porsche left.

He contemplated setting up his own company, but the time wasn't ripe – this, remember, was during the immediate post-World War One era when war reparations were crippling Germany's economy and inflation was growing out of control.

Instead Porsche took the position of technical director with Daimler, based in Stuttgart. Again, Daimler produced ostentatious luxury cars. Porsche himself designed some of the finest, including the tremendous 7.1-litre SS and SSK models of 1928. Most designers would have basked in the glory of such glamorous machines, but Porsche still harboured his down-to-earth ideals, and strived to get a small, utilitarian vehicle into production.

It was work on such a vehicle that brought simmering disagreements with other board members at Daimler (by now Daimler-Benz) to a head. The car in question was a 1,280cc front-engined design with swing-axle rear suspension. Thirty prototypes were built, but the board ultimately voted not to put it into production. In the resulting row Porsche resigned.

Disillusioned, he returned to Austria and joined Steyr. Again, he worked on the typical large-engined cars of the period, and designed the opulent 5.3-litre Austria, but the Wall Street Crash of 1929 hit Steyr hard. It was taken over by the same bank that controlled Austro-Daimler, and the companies eventually merged to form Steyr-Daimler-Puch. Porsche, whose bitter fall-out with Austro-Daimler in 1923 still rankled, decided his future lay elsewhere.

Economic conditions were not a lot more favourable than when Porsche had first contemplated setting up his own company, but by now he must have been feeling a considerable sense of frustration. He was fifty-five years old, and his long-dreamt-of small car was still to make the transition from imagination to reality. He now realized he would find it difficult to find a position of sufficient authority with an established motor manufacturer to get his ideas accepted. Porsche was widely acknowledged as one of the outstanding motor engineers of his generation, but the unbending nature of his personality, which had led to so many boardroom confrontations, made prospective employers wary of giving him too much authority within their hierarchies.

Boldly, Porsche took the decision to go it alone. At the end of 1930 he set up his motor design consultancy, the snappily titled *Dr Ing hc F Porsche GmbH Konstruktionsbüro für Motoren-Fahrzeug-, Luftfahrzeug-, und Wasserfahrzeugbau.* Which in translation meant that Porsche was also prepared to take on aeroplane and seaplane design to make ends meet.

Porsche moved his consultancy back to Stuttgart so as to be at the heart of the German motor industry. He took with him several high-flying engineers poached from

Steyr and Daimler-Benz, and put to work his son Ferry, who was then just twenty years old.

Commissions trickled in slowly. The first was a small car built for Wanderer, which was labelled Porsche Type 7 to hide the fact that the company was starting from scratch! In the styling of this car's curvaceous rear bodywork there was an unmistakable hint of the Beetle to come.

In August 1931 came another event of major historical significance for the Beetle, when Porsche was granted a patent for an independent car suspension system based on torsion bars. These were springs which worked by twisting, and they displayed several advantages over the traditional leaf spring. It took considerable development work before Porsche actually proved this ingeniously simple but effective

First real forerunner to the Beetle was the Type 12 prototype Porsche designed for Zündapp in 1932. From the side view in particular there are unmistakeable hints of the styling of the Beetle to come.

system in action, and it ultimately formed the basis for the Beetle's suspension. Torsion bar suspension systems were taken up by several other manufacturers, so Porsche received some useful royalties.

Meanwhile, his company led a precarious existence. To fill in the gaps between commissions, and to fulfil his own ambitions, Porsche started sketching the designs for a speculative small car project – the Porsche Type 12.

PORSCHE TYPE 12

It was well-timed. Soon afterwards, in September 1931, Porsche met Dr Fritz Neumeyer, of Zündapp, a motorcycle manufacturer based in Nürnberg. Neumeyer had a proposition that was very close to Porsche's heart – a small car, cheap enough to appeal to his existing motorcycle customers. Zündapp were going through a

lean time of falling motorcycle sales, and saw the potential in this type of small car. Having no experience of building cars themselves, they turned to Porsche to design one for them. It was this car that was the first real forerunner to the Beetle.

His brief was for a four-seater passenger car with a two-door saloon body, swing-axle suspension and one-litre engine. The aim was a vehicle capable of returning an average fuel consumption of 35mpg (8.1l/100km) at an average speed of 40mph (65km/h).

Porsche knew that for the price Zündapp had in mind, such a vehicle would demand a radical rethink of construction techniques. The plans he came up with were a classic blend of simplicity and advanced engineering, and they bore a clear resemblance to the Beetle to come. The car was a rear-wheel drive design with a rear-mounted engine, clothed in a smooth, streamlined body shell.

Porsche also built a cabriolet version of the Type 12 prototype. Chopping off the top resulted in a square and less fluent design. Neither saloon or cabriolet ever made it past the prototype stage.

Porsche Type 12 (1932)

Engine

Type	Water-cooled five-cylinder radial
Capacity	1,200cc
Max. power	26bhp
Top speed	50mph (80km/h)

Transmission

Gearbox	Manual four-speed

Suspension

Front	Independent with transverse leaf spring
Rear	Independent with swing axles, radius arms, transverse leaf spring

---

As presented to Zündapp, the car even featured – like the Beetle – an air-cooled, four-cylinder boxer engine. But Zündapp's engineers overruled this, insisting that a water-cooled five-cylinder radial engine would be quieter.

Three prototypes were duly constructed. The Type 12 was certainly a small car, just 3.3m long, 1.42m wide, and 1.5m high. Its body, which with its curving roof is strongly reminiscent of the Beetle, was mounted on a hefty chassis, suspension being provided by transverse leaf springs on each of the swing axles. The 1.2-litre five-cylinder radial was good for an output of 26bhp, feeding through a three-speed plus overdrive transmission fitted in front of the engine. But on its first test run the Type 12 ran into overheating problems – because the radial engine was mounted in the tail, where it received little cooling air, it rapidly overheated and boiled over.

Such a problem was far from insurmountable, but the Type 12 failed to make it into production for other reasons – namely Zündapp's decision to stick to producing motorcycles once they'd considered more carefully the costs of setting a small car scheme in production. Sadly, none of the

three Zündapp prototypes survives. Zündapp may have scrapped the two they kept, while Porsche's surviving car was destroyed in an air raid on Stuttgart in 1944.

With the plans for his small car put on hold, Porsche's design company suffered another lean year in 1932. Thankfully, however, the idea was resuscitated in 1933 in collaboration with NSU.

NSU was another motorcycle firm who nevertheless did have some experience of making cars. When the bottom fell out of the car market during the Depression they had been forced to pass their car facility over to Italian firm Fiat. By 1933, however, the world – and German – economy was starting to look more healthy and NSU thought again about adding a car to their repertoire.

PORSCHE TYPE 32

NSU director Fritz von Falkenhayn gave Porsche a remarkably free hand in developing this car, which became Type 32 in Porsche's nomenclature. The Type 32 bore an even greater resemblance to the Beetle to come, with a tubular platform frame, an

With the 1933 Type 32 prototype, Porsche took another step towards the Beetle. This had an air-cooled flat-four engine in the tail, and torsion bars. Again, it never went into production.

Porsche Type 32 (1933–4)

Engine
Type	Flat-four, air-cooled
Capacity	1,470cc
Max. power	28bhp
Top speed	55mph (90km/h)

Transmission
Gearbox	Manual four-speed

Suspension
Front	Independent with transverse torsion bars and trailing arms
Rear	Independent with swing axles and torsion bars

air-cooled four-cylinder boxer engine mounted in the tail and a gearbox fitted in front of this in line with the rear axles. Porsche's patented torsion bars featured for the first time, fitted at the front and rear.

With its 1,470cc engine turning out some 28bhp, the Type 32, which weighed 750kg, was capable of a top speed of around 55mph (90km/h).

Three prototypes were built. One had a conventional steel body, whilst the other two were clothed in a mixture of wood and leather. Trials were completed in the Black Forest with surprisingly few hitches, although the noise from the air-cooled engine was deafening inside the cabin at high speed – 'Sounds like a broken-down bulldozer', commented von Falkenhayn. Occasionally this racket was supplemented by the gunshot-like retort of a torsion bar snapping, but these problems could be cured. Porsche immediately began experimenting with the metallurgy of the torsion bars to come up with a more durable formula.

For a time Porsche felt hopeful that at last his small car would go into production. But NSU, like Zündapp, were wary of venturing the high capital investment that would have been needed to put the Type 32 into production. Fiat also began to kick up a fuss about the prototype breaking an agreement they had made with NSU back in 1929, stating that NSU would no longer build cars. The project was shelved, NSU continued to concentrate on motorcycle production and, instead of a people's car, built a low-cost 'people's motorbike' – the NSU Quickly.

HITLER'S INVOLVEMENT

These two abortive projects had not been in vain, however. Porsche had turned his

---

Cars for the people

Today it's hard for us to imagine a society in which most adults don't have access to a car. Rising standards of living, combined with the cost-cutting permitted by mass-production, started to put a car within most people's grasp by the mid-1950s, and today driving is regarded more as a right than a privilege.

It wasn't always this way. At the turn of the century motor cars were strictly for the wealthy, and were considered playthings rather than essential transport. Cars were still made in much the same way as the ornate horse-drawn coaches they were slowly replacing – handbuilt by craftsmen. An individual wing might take eight hours of painstaking work to complete. This, and the small numbers of each model sold, meant cars were expensive to buy, and with unreliable early mechanicals, they cost a lot to maintain too.

Gradually cheaper cars started to appear. Many sported the successful one-cylinder engine built by French manufacturer De Dion. By selling this to many other manufacturers, as well as using it in their own cars, De Dion were able to make enough units to bring down costs and sell the engine cheaply. But the truly cheap cars were more often than not voiturettes – tiny, skimpy, vehicles which owed their design to motorcycle technology.

It was in America that the breakthrough came. Henry Ford designed the first proper small car for the masses – the Model T. A farmer's son who preferred engineering to farming, Ford moved to Detroit at the age of sixteen and built his first car in 1896. Ford's early designs were basic, but each model improved on the quality of the previous one. Ford aimed to produce a car that would be cheap enough to attract buyers who up till then had been limited to a horse and carriage, but which had a

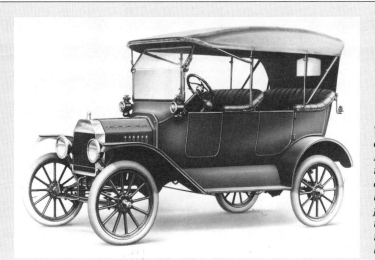

The original 'people's car', the Ford Model T. Priced so low it made Ford's own dealers blink, the legendary 'Tin Lizzie' put America on wheels, with more than fifteen million produced between 1908 and 1927.

comprehensive enough specification to appeal to them. The Model T, introduced in 1908, fitted the bill exactly.

With a side-valve, 2.9-litre, 20hp, four-cylinder engine driving a simple two-speed epicyclic gearbox, and a choice of two, four or five seats, the Model T was mechanically unremarkable. What was remarkable was its selling price. Henry Ford costed the Model T on the assumption that it would sell in vast numbers, and offered it at $850. Ford dealers could hardly believe this price when they heard it.

But Ford's gamble paid off. In 1909, 80,000 Model Ts sold. For the first time in the motor industry Henry Ford used techniques of mass-production, and in 1913 he introduced the moving assembly line. A Model T could now be put together in one and a half hours, enabling Ford to cut prices still further. In 1923 the year's sale total exceeded two million – all in black, of course – but soon afterwards time caught up with the Model T and sales slumped. Even so Ford refused to drop his beloved 'Tin Lizzie' until 1927, by which time an incredible 15,007,033 had been made.

But while owning a car was rapidly becoming the norm in America, events moved much more slowly on this side of the Atlantic, where large, expensive, chauffeur-driven cars were still the norm. Building a small, popular car was regarded as a very peculiar idea – and not a very profitable one at that. When Herbert Austin decided the market was ripe for a baby car – his Austin 7 – he had to design it at home after his work colleagues laughingly dismissed the idea.

This was an attitude Ferdinand Porsche was only too familiar with as he battled to get his vision of a people's car off the drawing board. As one baffled motor industrialist once said to him 'But Herr Porsche, what does each worker need his own car for? The people's car is a bus'.

When Porsche needed to learn about making small cars, it was natural he should go to America to visit Henry Ford and learn from his mass-production techniques. The two found they had a lot in common, and some lively conversation ensued. Porsche asked Ford if he was concerned that the German Volkswagen might one day be a threat to his sales. 'If someone else can build better and cheaper cars than I can', Ford retorted, 'then it serves me right!'

The Model T was a hard act to follow, and Porsche's Volkswagen took a while to recover from its shaky start in life, but ultimately it grew to match his vision. On 17 February 1972 the Beetle overtook the record sales figure established by the Model T 45 years before. Today, with the total production well over 21 million – and still rising – the Beetle has unquestionably earned the title of the ultimate people's car.

ideas for a people's car into real, practical, prototypes, and he was in a convincing position to argue that they should be developed further. There was now also another vital factor for Porsche to take into consideration: Adolf Hitler had become German Chancellor in January 1933, and he had declared himself in favour of making a small car that the mass of the population could afford to buy.

Porsche had met Hitler early in 1933 to persuade him to give state funding to an Auto-Union racing car that he was developing (this car went on to win three Grand Prix races in 1935). Hitler took a strong interest in motoring and showed great admiration for Porsche's achievements.

Hitler had an adviser on motoring matters in the figure of Jakob Werlin, a Munich Mercedes dealer who first sold Hitler a car in 1923. Since then his opinion had carried a lot of weight with Hitler. Werlin knew how much Hitler desired to see a cheap car made available to the German people, and he had also met Porsche and discovered his very similar ideas about a people's car. He advised Porsche to put his views down on paper. This Porsche duly did in a paper entitled *Ideas on the Construction of a German People's Car:*

> For years the German people have cherished the hope that they would be provided with a genuine people's car. Some cars of high quality have appeared on the market, but with prices incompatible with the average income. Such 'factory-produced people's cars' still tend to be designed for a limited class of buyer who will never and must never determine the future development of motorized transport.'

Porsche made it clear that although a people's car must be low-priced, it should still be built to the same standards as a proper car. He wrote:

> The manufacture of a standard radio set, the Volksempfänger (people's receiver), has shown the great economic significance of a product that combines high quality and outstanding value.
>
> A people's car should not be a small car which perpetuates the tradition of previous products in this range by simply exactly copying their pattern with reduced dimensions, power, weight and so forth. A vehicle such as this might be cheap in terms of its purchase price, but from the point of view of a healthy national economy it would be of little value because of its reduced passenger comfort and lifespan, and therefore in the long term it would be anything but cheap. In times of growth in traffic density, when safety is increasingly a priority, any suggestions of a sacrifice in quality on such a vehicle should be rejected.
>
> I would summarize the definition of a people's car as follows:
>
> 1) A people's car should not be a small car whose dimensions are reduced at the expense of handling and life expectancy, while it remains relatively heavy; instead, it should be a functional vehicle of normal dimensions but relatively low weight, a goal that can be achieved by fundamentally new processes.
>
> 2) A people's car should not be a small car with limited power at the expense of maximum speed and good climbing ability, but a fully practical vehicle which has the necessary power to achieve normal maximum speeds and climbing capability.
>
> 3) A people's car should not be a small car with reduced passenger space at the expense of comfort, but a fully functional vehicle with normal, comfortable, space within its bodywork.

4) A people's car should not be a vehicle with limited uses, but should be able to fulfil all conceivable purposes by simple exchange of bodywork, for use not only as a passenger vehicle but as a commercial vehicle and for certain military purposes.

5) A people's car should not be fitted with complex equipment requiring increased servicing, but should be a vehicle with as far as possible foolproof equipment, to reduce servicing to an absolute minimum.

On the basis of the observations set out above, the following qualities are demanded of the people's car:
– the best possible suspension and handling;
– a maximum speed of about 60mph (100km/h);
– a climbing ability of about thirty per cent
– closed four-seater bodywork for the transport of passengers;
– the lowest possible purchase price and running costs.

Based on these requirements, Porsche recommended the following specification:

Track	1,200mm
Wheelbase	2,500m
Max. power	26bhp
Max. engine speed	3,500rpm
Kerb weight	650kg
Selling price	RM1,550
Max speed	60mph (100km/h)
Climbing ability	30 per cent
Fuel consumption	35mpg (8.1l/100km)
Type of chassis	full swing axle

Porsche concluded his report with the comment that 'the construction of a people's car is especially close to my heart; all sections of the population have great expectations of this vehicle'.

Porsche presented copies of *Ideas on the Construction of a German People's Car* to Jakob Werlin, Adolf Hitler and the German Ministry of Transport on 17 January 1934, with the suggestion that the government should entrust him with the design of a people's car as a trial model. If this was successful, the government could then recommend that this model should be produced by the German motor industry.

Shortly afterwards Porsche received an invitation to meet Hitler at the Kaiserhof

Adolf Hitler – tyrant, madman, car enthusiast

Nazi leader Adolf Hitler was a man of obsessions. One of them was motoring – and as his obsessions went, this was one of the least offensive.

As early as 1923, when the German Nazi party was struggling to make ends meet, Hitler took a hefty chunk of its meagre funds to buy a 60hp Mercedes. He explained 'The automobile is for me but a means to an end. It alone makes it possible for me to accomplish my daily work'.

There was some truth in this. Like no politician ever before, Hitler used the car to span great distances between the Nazi rallies that were held throughout Germany between the wars. He also used the motor car to boost the nation's prestige. Money couldn't necessarily buy victory on the sports field, as black American Jesse Owens demonstrated when he dominated the running track in the 1936 Berlin Olympics, leaving the Nazi notion of racial superiority in tatters. Motor racing, however, was a safer bet. By pouring money into the Mercedes and Auto Union racing teams of the 1930s, Hitler could confidently ensure a string of German victories.

Like many of his other political ideas, Hitler's views on a car for the people, the 'Volkswagen', evolved during a brief spell of imprisonment following his unsuccessful attempt to overthrow the Bavarian government in the ill-planned 'beer-hall putsch' of November 1923.

While in Landsberg jail, Hitler read Henry Ford's autobiography *My Life and Work*, and admired Ford's efforts to produce an affordable small car. In *Mein Kampf*, which he also wrote at this time, Hitler talked of 'breaking the motoring privileges of the upper classes'.

Providing the German people with a car appealed to Hitler on a number of levels. For one, he genuinely believed that it could improve the lot of the average German worker. As Hitler proclaimed in his opening speech at the 1934 Berlin Motor Show, 'It is a bitter thought that millions of good and industrious people are excluded from the use of a means of transport that, especially on Sundays and holidays, could become for them a source of unknown joy'.

Adolf Hitler saw rich political dividends in making a cheap car available to the German people, but he loved cars for their own sake too. Here Ferdinand Porsche demonstrates a Beetle model to Hitler.

The political dividends of such a vehicle weren't to be overlooked either. A promise to provide the masses with transport would increase popular support for the Nazi regime, as would the thousands of jobs that would be provided for Germany's unemployed workers building the autobahn network needed for the people's new cars.

German national honour was at stake too. At that 1934 Motor Show, Hitler had complained that 'Germany has only one automobile for each 100 inhabitants. France has one for each 28 and the United States one for each six. That disparity must change'.

Hitler's wider ambitions of territorial expansion got in the way of his plans to bring motoring to the masses, and the outbreak of World War Two put an end to production of the Volkswagen before it had properly begun. It was ironic, too, that for all his enthusiasm for motoring, Hitler never actually learned to drive – he had to be chauffeur-driven everywhere. But the most ironic twist of all for Hitler was that the only long drive he ever took in a Volkswagen was his last ever journey in a vehicle – to the Berlin bunker where he ended his life in suicide. He chose a Volkswagen for the trip as it was less conspicuous than his usual Mercedes limousine.

Hotel in Berlin. This historic meeting took place in May 1934.

Over afternoon tea Hitler swiftly outlined his own view of a people's car. It should, he declared, have five seats, an air-cooled engine, be capable of cruising at a steady 60mph (100km/h), and return 40mpg (7.1l/100km). All of this was much in keeping with Porsche's own views. But when Porsche enquired what price Hitler had in mind for such a car, he was flabbergasted by the reply: 'At any price, Herr Dr

Porsche. At any price, that is, below 1,000 Marks!'

At the time this was about the price of a medium-sized motorbike. The cheapest Ford cost three times as much, even though it employed the latest mass-production techniques. To Porsche it seemed nonsense to suggest that a car could be built so cheaply, and he went home from his meeting with Hitler a discouraged man. But the ideal of a people's car burnt fiercely within Porsche. If he didn't take this opportunity to build a people's car with Hitler's powerful backing, would another chance ever come along?

Porsche resolved to accept the challenge. He drew up a prototype people's car heavily Beetle-like in design, which he named the Type 60. Hitler gave his approval to these plans and passed the project into the authority of the German Automobile Industry Association (RDA). In June 1934 Porsche signed a contract with the RDA to undertake the development of a people's car.

There were a few drawbacks. Although they were nominally in charge of the project, the RDA had no interest in seeing it succeed. Why, they felt, should they help promote a state-supported car which would certainly damage the profitability of their own manufacturers' models? They granted Porsche a meagre RM233,000 (£20,000), told him to produce three prototypes, and gave him an absurdly short ten-month deadline. He had no special facilities beyond the double garage of his home in Stuttgart. Meanwhile, Hitler was still insistent that the car should sell for just 990 Reichsmarks (around £85 at the time), a sum which by Porsche's own calculations was impossibly low.

The seas ahead looked choppy. But Ferdinand Porsche was happy – his Volkswagen was on its way.

2 Birth of the Volkswagen

V1 AND V2 PROTOTYPES

Ferdinand Porsche's small team set to work on the first batch of prototypes in his small garage workshop. Working conditions were far from ideal. His son Ferry, then aged twenty-five, recalls in his memoirs: 'We used my hobby workshop, installed two lathes along with the existing milling machine and pillar drill and then found room enough for twelve men. Don't ask me how we did it . . .'

Porsche labelled the prototypes Porsche Type 60. However, they were also given separate Volkswagen-type reference numbers and to avoid confusion these are the ones we shall stick with. There was to be a saloon, type number V1, as well as a cabriolet version, type V2 (the V stood for *Versuch,* experimental). Porsche was freer now than ever to bring his personal concept of a people's car to fruition, and the V1 naturally evolved from the Type 32 design he had produced for NSU. It was to be a rear-engined, air-cooled vehicle with torsion bar suspension.

It's worth taking a look at Porsche's reasoning behind this line of development. At this time, remember, the vast majority of vehicles were front-engined with rear-wheel drive.

Front-wheel drive, which now dominates the motoring scene, was in the early 1930s used only by a few oddball pioneers. The additional complication of combining steering and driven wheels added greatly to complexity, and Porsche would have rejected it as too costly and unreliable for his utilitarian vehicle. But he did see the logic of having the engine and the driven wheels at the same end of the car. Why, he asked, put the engine at one end and then connect it to the wheels at the other with a prop-shaft? This shaft only added expense and weight, and, because it had to be housed in a transmission tunnel, ate into the passenger space available inside the car.

Porsche described in his paper *Ideas on the Construction of a German People's Car* the advantages of a rear-engined configuration – 'unlimited use of the length of the vehicle, allowing favourable positioning of the seats; no intermediate shaft, hence low intrinsic weight; good accessibility and repairability; vibration-free positioning; no road noise or engine smells within the car'.

That the engine should be air-cooled also made a great deal of sense to Porsche. A water-cooled engine needed a separate radiator (which meant more weight and expense), and was likely to be less reliable, boiling over in hot weather and freezing in the cold. This last point was important considering the target market for the people's car. The average German worker was unlikely to have a garage in which to keep his car overnight. It would have to be left on the street at the mercy of the elements during Germany's bitter winters. In temperatures which would freeze solid a

An early version of the air-cooled flat-four designed by Franz Reimspeiss. Air-cooling was a natural choice, as it meant there was no danger of the engine freezing up during Germany's harsh winter nights.

had set. He experimented with a number of two-stroke engine designs on the basis that they would be cheaper to produce than a four-stroke. Both a twin-cylinder boxer and a three-cylinder radial were considered, and several variations on the two-stroke theme were tried in the V1 prototype. None proved satisfactory, however. The biggest difficulty was building a two-stroke that would perform reliably at the 60mph (100km/h) motorway cruising speed specified. In all, some twenty experimental engines were built, tested and discarded.

Finally, the solution was supplied by one Franz Reimspeiss, a 33-year-old engineer who, like Porsche, had gained a grounding in his trade at Austro-Daimler. Reimspeiss took on the task of designing a four-cylinder engine for the V1, and in a flash of genius he rapidly produced a sketch of the engine that was to form the heart of millions of Volkwagens. When costed, the engine actually proved cheaper to manufacture than any of the two-stroke options. It was light, simple and very rugged, and as Porsche himself pointed out, would be more suitable for export than a two-stroke.

For suspension, Porsche's own patented independent system using torsion bars was the obvious choice. Superior to the leaf springs fitted to most cars of the period, torsion bars enclosed in tubes were more compact, weighed less, were better protected from the elements and operated in a more sophisticated fashion. Torsion bars have the major advantage of deforming progressively in relation to the force applied to them. The more the bar is twisted, the stiffer it becomes. This means that while the torsion bar system could cope admirably with rough, potholed tracks, it would still deliver a supple, comfortable ride over smoother roads. Torsion bars were also more effective than leaf springs in preventing the wheels from hopping

water-cooled engine, an air-cooled one would be ready to take off into the frosty dawn at the first touch on the starter (or, more likely with an early six-volt Beetle, the first crank of the starting handle).

On the downside, an air-cooled engine would inevitably be noisier than a water-cooled one, primarily because it lacks a sound-deadening jacket of water, but also because its internal tolerances have to be larger. But to Porsche this small disadvantage seemed well outweighed by the benefits of air-cooling.

While this fundamental point of specification was easily settled, the details of the engine design remained a subject of fierce discussion well into the production of prototypes. Porsche was continually forced to deviate from what he knew to be the most sensible course because of the need to keep the selling price of the Volkswagen within the seemingly unrealistic limits that Hitler

Porsche's patented torsion bar suspension system offered a number of advantages – not least that it could be housed within solid metal tubes, safe from damage and protected from corrosion.

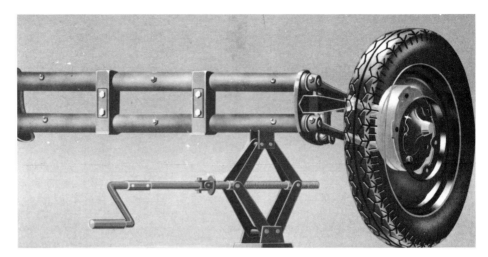

The Beetle combines lightness with strength, thanks to its central backbone – which also provides a handy route for control cables. However, it isn't fully rigid without the body bolted in place.

while going round bumpy corners, and they reduced the degree of roll.

The torsion bar set-up was refined from the one fitted to the Type 32. At the front there were now two tubes, each containing a torsion bar, instead of the single tube containing twin torsion bars which featured on the Type 32. This spread the load more evenly and reduced wear rates.

In contrast to most cars of the time, which featured a hefty girder chassis with bodywork simply tacked on top, the floor-pan for the Beetle prototype was a much more sophisticated design. It had a central backbone which provided most of the strength (and also gave a handy route for the various control cables and wires), but it also relied on the body of the car, once bolted securely into place, contributing its own fair share to the assembly's overall rigidity. Because the chassis didn't provide all the stiffness, it could be made a lot lighter than the usual girder-type chassis designs.

Meanwhile, work continued on honing the Beetle's distinctive shape. Streamlining was the big influence, both in practical and political terms. To an engineer like Porsche, streamlined bodywork meant lower wind resistance, a higher top speed and better fuel consumption. To the Nazis, streamlining symbolized the best in modern and efficient design trends, a harmony of form with function. Germany was at the forefront of aerodynamic research in the 1930s, and Porsche was clearly influenced by such vehicles as Edmund Rumpler's teardrop-shaped Tropfenwagen of 1921. He himself had successfully applied streamlining techniques to the Austro-Daimler Prince Heinrich racing car of 1910 in a bid to increase its competitiveness.

There has been some debate over the degree of inspiration that Porsche took from a company making cars across the border in Czechoslovakia. Tatra was run by another exuberantly innovative engineer, Hans Ledwinka, who since the turn of the century had been producing cars with strikingly streamlined bodywork – and air-cooled, rear-mounted engines. The Tatra Type 570 prototype had an 850cc rear-mounted twin-cylinder engine in bodywork that bore a remarkable resemblance to Porsche's later Volkswagen prototypes.

Tatras were also popular transport with high-ranking Nazis. Hitler had been driven around extensively in a Type 11 during the 1920s, and the experience had cemented his enthusiasm for rear-engined cars.

Porsche undoubtedly took note of Ledwinka's ideas, and admitted once that 'sometimes I looked over his shoulder and sometimes he looked over mine'. But it would be wrong to accuse Porsche of blatant plagiarism. He was just one of a group of central European engineers exploring similar themes which at that time were at the cutting edge of car design.

In 1938 Germany occupied Czechoslovakia, took over the Tatra works, and from then on some Tatra technology unarguably did find its way onto the Volkswagen. Hans Ledwinka protested against the patent infringements he saw taking place, but the Nazi regime shrugged off his complaints. Volkswagen did eventually make a settlement in 1967, paying Tatra DM3 million in damages. Ironically, this was the same year that Hans Ledwinka died, almost penniless, aged 89.

Mainly because of the difficulties he had encountered arriving at a suitable engine design, Porsche ran well past his ten-month deadline. He was also still arguing with the RDA about the cost of the Volkswagen. Hitler had been adamant that the car should sell for no more than RM1,000. But Porsche stubbornly stuck to his aim of building a proper, soundly-built, small car, and he calculated this would cost more than RM1,400. To build a cheaper car would, he argued heatedly, mean lowering standards to an unacceptable level.

During this period Porsche was clearly trying to keep the RDA at arm's length. In turn, an internal memo circulated to the board of the RDA, and dated 5 February 1936, was sharply critical of Porsche's working methods. It chafed at his delays, particularly the nine months that Porsche had lost trying to develop the abortive two-stroke engine, and made it clear that he was not keeping to the price limits laid down by Adolf Hitler. 'Producing a car costing RM1,600, or even RM1,500, would not be in accordance with the Führer's intention at all, since cars are already available in this price category', complained the memo.

Tellingly, the memo continued in a vein that reflected the RDA's main consideration at this time – protecting its members' interests against a state-subsidized car. It noted that the preparations for the Volkswagen had already encouraged Opel and Auto Union to reduce the prices of their small car models – if the Volkswagen were to appear for RM1,400 or more, it would 'split the market and none of the three factories would stand a chance of producing in sufficient numbers'.

VW3

Despite the wrangling, Porsche was given the go-ahead to build a further run of three more prototypes in order to perfect his design. They were designated VW3s.

To today's eyes the VW3 is recognizably a Beetle, though one still several design stages away from the finished product. Rear-opening 'suicide doors' (so called

because of the danger of them flying open while driving if not securely fastened) were fitted, there was no rear window, and only the top half of the front bonnet was designed to open. The headlamps sat, frog-eye-like, lower down on the bonnet. The power unit was Reimspeiss's flat-four.

Only one of the VW3 prototypes was fitted with a steel bodyshell, the other pair being clothed in a combination of wood and steel. Porsche had been considering employing a timber-framed body clothed with sheet metal panels in order to reduce production costs, but ultimately he decided that in view of the Volkswagen's anticipated lifestyle – being left outside in all weathers rather than pampered in a warm dry garage – such a construction would not be robust enough. Light alloy bodywork was also considered, but on the grounds of cost

The Beetle takes shape in an early prototype, the VW3 of 1935/6. This model had an air-cooled flat-four engine and torsion bar suspension, but, unlike the Beetle to come, it featured 'suicide' doors, headlamps mounted on the bonnet, and lacked a rear window.

VW3 (Porsche Type 60) (1935–6)

Engine
Type	Air-cooled flat-four
Capacity	984cc
Maximum power	22bhp
Top speed	60mph (100km/h)

Transmission
Gearbox	Manual four-speed

Suspension
Front	Independent with transverse torsion bars and trailing arms
Rear	Independent with swing axles, and torsion bars

Dimensions
Weight	1,430lb (650kg)

the final decision was for an all-steel body.

In October 1936 the VW3 prototypes were finally ready to show their mettle. They were handed over to the RDA, who had devised a rigorous testing schedule.

The cars covered a daily 700km (435 mile) test run, taking in a variety of terrains including stiff climbs in the Black Forest and high-speed stretches of autobahn. Each car covered in excess of 48,000km (30,000 miles), mostly in wretched weather during the onset of winter. Every aspect of the cars' performance was the subject of minutely detailed observations. Notes for car number one on 28 November revealed 'a slight knock coming from the engine, the car then travelling at 53mph (85km/h); about 40 minutes afterwards at 3.27pm a very loud knock was heard and the engine started to run irregularly. The car was stopped immediately and it was found that the connecting rod of the third cylinder was broken and had penetrated through the crankcase. After examination it was found that the rod failed due to faulty materials. See attached metallur-

gical report and photographs'.

Thousands of reports like this were analysed, and in January the RDA released a detailed report on their progress.

Such intensive testing had thrown up a few weaknesses in the VW3's design, but these were no more than might have been expected, and none was serious. The most significant modification needed was to the engine crankshaft. The original cast-iron component failed repeatedly, and was replaced by a tougher forged crankshaft. Electric fuel pumps had also proved troublesome, so mechanical pumps were substituted. The front suspension and cable brakes also came in for some criticism.

The conclusion, written in carefully worded language by RDA technical officer Herr Vorwig, stated: 'The general performance and roadholding characteristics of the vehicle have proved on the whole entirely satisfactory. Based on these observations it would seem advisable to consider the continuation of the development of this vehicle'. Vorwig had reason to pick his words with care – on the one hand the VW3

Beetle prototypes went through an exhaustive testing regime closer to modern procedures than the standards of the day. Here the first prototypes, the V1 and V2 cabriolet, are put through their paces.

was Hitler's pet project and he'd be taking a close interest in the report, and on the other the RDA had been hoping – and confidently expecting – that the prototypes would fall to bits during the testing procedure, allowing their pieces to be conveniently swept under the carpet.

As Vorwig commented in 1949, by which time he was secretary-general of the RDA's postwar replacement, *Verband der Automobilindustrie:*

At the time it was obvious to me that private industry could not have any interest in the development of the Volkswagen, creating competition against their own products. But to express such an opinion or even refer to it in the report was not my

duty as the technical officer of the society.

But the RDA did continue to criticize Porsche's design on the grounds of cost – they couldn't see how such a vehicle could be produced for Hitler's stated RM990. Once again, the president of the RDA revealed his association's true interests when he suggested that instead of adopting Porsche's design, there should be a competition among German car companies to produce a people's car. This was the final straw for Hitler, who had long grown impatient with the delays and the lukewarm enthusiasm of the RDA. Now he suspected a conspiracy, using American money to steal the people's car project out of German hands, and turn it over to US-funded

Berlin–Rome Racer

Ferdinand Porsche was always fascinated by motor racing. As much as he personally enjoyed the excitement of motorsport, Porsche also firmly believed that racing had an important role to play in developing and improving car designs. So, not surprisingly, while he was developing the Volkswagen prototypes he made repeated requests to be allowed to produce a sporting version to test on the track.

These requests were invariably turned down by the DAF, accompanied by the discouraging comment that a sports car was not a car for the people, and was therefore irrelevant to the Volkswagen project.

It took more than this to quench Porsche's enthusiasm, and he carried out a number of development exercises to determine the sporting potential of the Volkswagen. Twin carburettors, superchargers and fuel injection were all tried to see what improvements they could make to the power output of the flat-four engine. Drawings for an aerodynamic coupé were also produced, some showing a modified engine mounted in the middle of the chassis instead of at the rear.

Porsche's chance to put these ideas into practice came with the announcement of a road-race that was planned to run from Berlin to Rome during September 1939. Eager as ever to demonstrate Aryan superiority through motor racing, Nazi officials swiftly changed their minds about the appropriateness of a racing Volkswagen, and they commissioned Porsche to build a car specifically for this event.

Porsche dug out his old designs and began work on the Porsche Type 64, or Berlin–Rome Racer. Its flat-four engine was bored out to 1,100cc, and tweaked to give 40bhp. Braking and suspension, however, were kept surprisingly unaltered.

More effort was applied to the design of the bodywork. The first 350 miles of the event were to be run flat-out on the autobahn from Berlin to Munich, so aerodynamic efficiency would be of paramount importance. Consequently, the Berlin–Rome racer was given strikingly streamlined coupé bodywork which completely enveloped the chassis and tapered upwards into a tiny cabin. Weight too was pared down from the standard car's 650kg to just 545kg. The resulting vehicle was capable of an impressive top speed (considering its power output) nudging 90mph (145km/h).

One drawback was that space inside the racer was desperately tight. The driver sat almost centrally, with a passenger seat squeezed in at an angle behind him.

The outbreak of war meant the cancellation of the Berlin–Rome race, and just three racers were built. Porsche used one as a runabout during the war, but this was requisitioned by occupying US servicemen and fell to bits soon afterwards. Another, however, survived the war and afterwards competed successfully in the hands of an Austrian racing driver.

War prevented the Type 64 from running in the Berlin to Rome race it was designed for. Based on largely standard Beetle mechanicals, its 40bhp engine in heavily streamlined bodywork gave a top speed nudging 90mph (145km/h).

companies Opel or Ford. His response was to bring the RDA's responsibility for the Volkswagen to an end. He moved the project within the Nazi establishment, where it would be given top priority.

Opel did in fact press on with plans to design a small car, the P4. This was revealed at the 1937 Motor Show, labelled 'the car for the small man' and priced RM1,450. Waiting at the stand to welcome Hitler was Willhelm von Opel. 'And this, my Führer, is *our* Volkswagen' he proudly declared. Hitler, enraged that Opel, with the aid of American finance, should have pre-empted his own people's car, turned away and stalked off in a rage. Two weeks later an order was passed establishing government control over the supply of iron and steel. Try as they might, Opel executives couldn't get their applications passed for these essential raw materials they desperately needed to build their 'people's car'.

Meanwhile, responsibility for development of the Volkswagen had passed to Hitler's pet German Workers Front, the DAF, headed by the shambling, alcoholic

Nazi, Dr Robert Ley. This organization had replaced the outlawed trade unions and seized their funds, which were now smartly channelled into the Volkswagen project. An additional 'contribution' came from the German workforce in the shape of an extra 1.5 per cent on income tax.

On 28 May 1937, a separate entity was set up to oversee the project. This was the *Gessellschaft zur Vorbereitung des Volkswagens* (Society for the Development of the Volkswagen), popularly known by its shortened name, Gesuvor. Headed by high-ranking Nazi Dr Bodo Lafferentz, Gesuvor immediately received a transfer of RM500,000 (£43,000) from the DAF, and they ordered a further batch of prototypes from Ferdinand Porsche.

VW30

These were designated VW30, and they moved the Volkswagen concept one step nearer to its final form. Headlamps were moved to the front wings, though they were

---

Berlin–Rome racer (Type 64) (1939)

Engine

Type	Air-cooled flat-four
Capacity	1,100cc
Max. power	40bhp
Top speed	90mph (145km/h)

Tranmission

Gearbox	Manual four-speed

Suspension

Front	Independent with transverse torsion bars and trailing arms
Rear	Independent with swing axles and torsion bars

Dimensions

Weight	1,201lb (545kg)

The VW30 prototype looked much closer to the Beetle in its final form, though a rear window was still conspicuously absent. Thirty of these cars underwent a massive testing programme in the hands of the SS, covering a total of 1.5 million miles.

VW30 1936–7

Engine
Type	Air-cooled flat-four
Capacity	985cc
Max. power	23bhp
Top speed	60mph (100km/h)

Transmission
Gearbox	Manual four-speed

Suspension
Front	Independent with transverse torsion bars and trailing arms
Rear	Independent with swing axles and torsion bars

Dimensions
Weight	1,430lb (650kg)

---

not yet sloped to sit flush with the bodywork. The overall body contours looked very Beetle-like, although, inconveniently for whoever was driving, there was still no rear window. This, plus the fact that most VW30s were not fitted with bumpers, gave the VW30 a sleek, sculpted, appearance which makes it aesthetically an extremely pure expression of the Beetle. Power was supplied by the 985cc flat-four engine, and suspension by the familiar torsion bar system. Brakes were drum all-round. One of the 30 prototypes sported an open-top body.

The VW30 prototypes embarked on a massive programme of testing. They were taken to the SS barracks at Kornwestheim, near Stuttgart, where 120 SS men were given the task of driving them over a punishing schedule, ultimately racking up an astonishing combined total of 1.5 million miles. Nowadays it's taken for granted that a motor manufacturer will put any new model through high-mileage testing, but in the 1930s such a trial was unheard of. By the time the SS had finished with them, there were few doubts about the Volkswagen's ruggedness and reliability.

Mechanically, the car was now proven and it just remained for Porsche's body stylist, Erwin Komenda, to make some small but significant revisions to the bodywork. Doors were altered so they hinged more safely at the front instead of the rear edges, and the front bonnet was formed in a single piece, hinged at the bulkhead. A rear window was at last fitted – or rather two small kidney-shaped panes of flat glass that were to give early Beetles their characteristic 'split-window' appearance. Small running boards were added, two strips of vertical cooling louvres were placed in the bodywork above the engine cover and hubcaps were fitted.

VW38

These revisions were all incorporated in the final run of 44 prototypes, named the VW38 series. This was the Beetle in its final form, but it couldn't actually be built

Wolfsburg – factory and town

The town of Wolfsburg, as it is known today, began life in 1938 as KdF-Stadt (Strength Through Joy Town). It was to be a model settlement, with the Volkswagen factory located next door to its own satellite town, where its workers would live and play.

Building an entire town from scratch is no small undertaking – but it does help if you have a dictatorship backing the project. The job of finding a site for the town went to Dr Bodo Lafferentz, head of Gesuvor, and he took to the skies in an aeroplane and cruised round looking for a suitable location. The spot he chose was in the heart of Germany, near to the small village of Fallersleben, some 25 miles (40km) from Brunswick.

Several things attracted Lafferentz to the area. Firstly, there was its central position in the German state. Secondly, communications were excellent – the factory could be built right next to the Mittelland Canal, while the main Berlin to Hanover autobahn ran nearby. Thirdly, there was a plentiful labour supply in the district. And finally, the area was one of natural beauty, as befitted a model town that would be a showpiece for the nation.

Not everyone was pleased with the choice. Particularly unenthusiastic was one Count von der Schulenburg, who owned most of the land on which the town was to be built. The Count's family had been presented with their land by Emperor Lothar II back in 1135, and not unnaturally he wasn't keen to give it up. He argued on a number of grounds that the site was unsuitable, finally, in desperation, claiming that the area was infested with mosquitoes. In fact, this turned out to be true, but the Count's last line of defence didn't last long, as an entomologist was called in, identified twenty-odd species of mosquito and exterminated the lot of them.

Town plans were drawn up by architect Peter Koller. The Nazi's favourite architect, Albert Speer, would have been the natural choice, but he was too busy remodelling Berlin along predictably monumental lines. Koller, a committed Christian, included two churches in his plan, but these were later struck out by Hitler.

Work on the site started in February 1938, and Hitler laid the foundation stone of the Volkswagen factory on 26 May. From then on work proceeded rapidly. The full plans included a power station, glass and rubber factories, steelworks, and a car testing circuit.

However, preparations for war soon began to take priority over building a car factory. About 3,000 construction workers were transferred to work on the Siegfried Line fortifications. Then, in autumn 1939, just as car production was about to start, the Reich Air Ministry requisitioned the plant and it became part of the German war effort.

This made it an enemy target, and Allied bombing raids in 1944 destroyed two-thirds of the factory. After the war the division of Germany left the factory within sight of the watchtowers and barbed wire fences of the East German border. But with the resumption of Beetle production, Wolfsburg quickly became, as had been originally intended, the largest car factory in Europe.

A journalist from the *Economist*, visiting in 1953, found:

a well-laid out production unit hidden behind a remarkable administrative block, nearly a mile long, with several floors of offices, halls, canteens, to seat 9,500 people at once, and a long 'kibitzers' gallery' along which sightseers can view the huge press shop, bodywork department and assembly hall from above. It is well-equipped with overhead conveyor belts and power tools for the men working on the line – the press shop, now overcrowded and needing new space, is one of the largest in Europe; and a large proportion of its machine tools have been installed or renewed since the war. Its production lines at present roll off a VW under its own power every minute and a half.

By 1968 the Wolfsburg factory employed 48,000 people, covered 384 acres, had more than 10,000 production machines and 40 miles (64km) of railway track and possessed its own

VW's Wolfsburg factory has a mile-long frontage alongside the Mittelland Canal. Despite suffering extensive damage during the war, by the early 1950s it had grown into the largest car factory in Europe, with a Beetle leaving its production lines every 90 seconds.

1.1-mile (1.7km) test track plus the most modern wind tunnel facility in Europe, capable of simulating 110mph (177km/h) winds and temperatures from -40°C to +60°C. Beetle production at Wolfsburg finally ceased in July 1974 to free the production lines for the new generation of Golfs and Polos.

As for Wolfsburg itself, it started to gain independence from the factory in 1952 when Volkswagen donated DM9.5million to provide basic municipal facilities in the town. Links between factory and town have always remained close, however – VW has since built an Olympic swimming pool in the town and assisted with the construction of a town hall, cultural centre and planetarium.

Ironically, considering its origins, Wolfsburg is notably free from traffic, with many pedestrianized streets. Its 130,000 inhabitants can enjoy a quiet stroll down the high street, called – what else – Porschestrasse.

yet – Hitler didn't even lay the foundation stone to the Volkswagen factory until 26 May 1938. And no one yet called it the Beetle. Hitler, at that same stone-laying ceremony, had announced for the very first time his name for the people's car.

'This car', he proclaimed, 'is being built for the broad masses. It meets their needs and should bring them joy. This car can have only one name, which I will give it today. It should have the name of the orga-nization that has worked the hardest for the broad mass of our people with joy and strength. It will be called the Kraft-durch-Freude-Wagen'.

On hearing this the assembled crowd of Nazi officials, Hitler Youth and associated sycophants cheered wildly. Meanwhile, Ferdinand Porsche, dressed as ever in his civilian togs, looked askance at what has certainly gone down as the daftest name for a car in automotive history. Most people

Stylist Erwin Komenda made a few revisions to the bodywork to arrive at the VW38, a final run of 44 prototypes that were in all essentials the completed Beetle – but at this time there wasn't even a factory to build it in.

VW38 (KdF-Wagen) (1937–9)

Engine

Type	Air-cooled flat-four
Capacity	985cc
Maximum power	23bhp
Top speed	60mph (100km/h)

Transmission

Gearbox	Manual four-speed

Suspension

Front	Independent with transverse torsion bars and trailing arms
Rear	Independent with swing axles, transverse torsion bars

Dimensions

Weight	1,445lb (655kg)

sensibly ignored the 'Strength-through-Joy' title and continued to refer to the car as the Volkswagen.

In a one-party state you don't need to worry much about slick marketing, and whatever its name there was a great demand for the as yet unproduced Volkswagen. Germans in their thousands started laying down a weekly deposit in their Volkswagen savings book. Gesuvor chief Bodo Lafferentz helped boost their enthusiasm by parading processions of KdF-Wagens through German towns.

Not that any of these prospective customers ever received a car. Some 210 KdF-Wagens were built before the outbreak of

An interior shot of the KdF-wagen from an early sales brochure, showing the 'cog-wheel' VW logo in its original form, stamped on the car radio set which was offered to buyers as an extra-cost option.

Porsche designed an ingenious heating system for his Volkswagen. Air was sucked in through the engine lid vents, warmed as it passed over the engine, and then channelled through the sills into the car.

A series of processions through German cities whetted the public's appetite for their new people's car.

An open-top Beetle was always part of the plan. This 1938 convertible, looking rather uninviting in the snow, was the forerunner to the Hebmüller and Karmann Cabrios launched after the war.

43

Saloon, cabriolet and saloon with full-length sunroof line up at the Volkswagen factory opening ceremony, at which Adolf Hitler (on podium) proudly announced the car's name – Kraft-durch-Freude-Wagen.

Buying a Beetle with saving stamps

By the middle of 1938 Germans were full of eagerness to get their hands on the people's car that had been promised them. Two problems stood in the way. The first was that the German Labour Front (DAF) had yet to put the car into production, and before it could it would have to underwrite the vast investment needed to set the production lines rolling.

The second was that most German workers couldn't afford the Volkswagen anyway. A price tag of RM990 might have been well below the going rate for a small car, but the average German worker simply didn't have this amount of money tucked away under the mattress.

The solution, as proposed by the DAF's Dr Robert Ley on 1 August 1938, was a scheme of astounding inventiveness, simplicity, and – to a modern viewpoint – barefaced cheek. Ley announced that all German citizens, regardless of class, status or property, might buy a VW. To do so, they had to purchase a savings card (costing one Reichsmark) and each week add a minimum of one RM5 saving stamp to it. Save

Few German citizens could afford to buy a Beetle outright – so they were encouraged to save up for one by collecting savings stamps. Stamps cost RM5, and the total cost of a Beetle, including delivery and insurance, was RM1,240.

the total of RM990 and they could proudly drive away in a brand new Volkswagen.

Actually, it turned out they'd need a bit more than the RM990 price tag that Hitler had insisted on, as there was the RM50 delivery charge, plus RM200 to cover the first two years' compulsory insurance. In addition, savers could also get supplementary cards worth RM60, which covered the extra cost of a car radio or a full-length fabric sunroof.

Walk into any car dealer today and you'll be bombarded with special purchase schemes, 0% finance and drive-now-pay-later-deals. If a salesman suggested that you pay by instalments, all up front and earning no interest, with a nasty non-cancellation clause thrown in for good measure, and after all that he couldn't even guarantee a delivery date, he'd be laughed off the forecourt.

But to Germany's car-hungry public the scheme looked a bargain. Ignoring the war clouds gathering ominously on the horizon, an astonishing 270,000 savers came forward to put down their first deposit. That figure was more than twice Opel's annual production at the time, and it guaranteed a large and steady market for the Volkswagen for some years to come. Even after war had been declared savers continued to enlist. By the end of the war the total of participants had reached 336,638, and RM267million had been lodged with the German Worker's Bank.

This was an enormous sum of money, which helped buffer Germany's economy during the war years. But not one of those savers received the car they'd painstakingly saved for.

So successful was the savings scheme as a means of raising money that at the time some commentators considered the whole Volkswagen scheme to be nothing more than a giant confidence trick, aimed at extracting money from the German people to fund Hitler's expansionist policies. Although in hindsight it doesn't seem that the savings scheme was quite so cynical an exercise, what is certain is that in the aftermath of the war there was a large body of savers demanding increasingly loudly that they be given the car they'd paid for.

Of the original 330,000 participants, 144,000 maintained a claim after the war – although three-quarters of these still simply wanted to get their new VW as promised. Largely because it was unclear who actually owned the Volkswagen concern after the war, their claim dragged on for years. After the privatization of VW in 1960, the case went to the courts. In light of the postwar currency reform that decimated the value of savings in Germany, it looked unlikely that the claimants would receive compensation in full – quite apart from the fact that this would have crippled Volkswagen financially.

Finally, the courts ruled that participants in the KdF savings scheme were eligible for a discount of up to DM600 on a new VW (then priced about DM4,000), or cash compensation of up to DM100. In the end some 80,000 people qualified for this long-awaited settlement, more than twenty years after the savings scheme had been first announced.

WER SIND DIE

Dr. Ley hat bekannt gegeben, daß die Volkswagenfabrik in Fallersleben keine Volkswagen herstellen wird. Die Beiträge jedoch sind weiter zu bezahlen.

PLUTOKRATEN?

This propaganda leaflet, dropped on wartime Germany by Allied aeroplanes, aimed to sow discontent by implying that the Nazi regime had no intention of making the Volkswagens that German citizens were saving for.

war, and all of them went to high-ranking party officials. On 1 September 1939, Germany invaded Poland. Hitler had embarked on his six year campaign of war,

misery and chaos, and the Volkswagen factory would have more pressing concerns on its hands producing arms for the military than cars for the people.

3 Volkswagen at War

Hitler came to power in 1933 with the avowed aim of re-arming Germany and turning it once more into a powerful military nation. As the 1930s progressed the armed forces played an increasingly wide role in all areas of society. It was inevitable that their eyes would fall on the newly conceived Volkswagen, considering whether it had military as well as civilian potential.

Serious scrutiny of the Volkswagen for military purposes began during the testing of the VW30 prototypes by the SS – one VW30 chassis was modified with rudimentary bodywork on which three seats and a machine gun were bolted.

This idea came to nothing, but the following year the German army, the Wehrmacht, asked Porsche to design a military multi-purpose vehicle based on the KdF-Wagen. The KdF-Wagen was an obvious choice in several respects: its air-cooled engine could operate in any theatre of war from the Arctic to the tropics; with the weight of its engine over the driven wheels, it had excellent traction in boggy conditions; and the engine was highly accessible for maintenance and was designed to keep running with the minimum of attention.

The result was the Porsche Type 62, which became known as the Kübelwagen (this seemingly unflattering title – bucket car – referred to the seat design, not the vehicle as a whole).

Mechanical parts for the military Volkswagen came directly from the KdF-Wagen. Bodywork was simple, lightweight and utilitarian. Occupants were open to the skies, though there was a rudimentary hood that could be raised to keep most of the weather out. Doors were simple affairs made of canvas.

Early trials of the Kübelwagen resulted in a few significant changes. Steel doors were fitted, and the slab-like body panels were ribbed to provide extra strength. In use the Kübelwagen proved tough, practical and manoeuvrable. But it met criticism on a couple of counts. Firstly, its cross-country ability was not as good as had been hoped, and was further hampered by the vehicle's relatively limited ground clearance. Secondly, the gearbox ratios were too high, even in bottom gear, for the Kübelwagen to be driven slowly enough to match the pace of a column of marching soldiers.

Porsche came up with an ingenious solution to these problems: fitting reduction gears inside the rear hubs. This had the dual effect of raising the Kübel's ground clearance, while lowering the overall gearing so that the vehicle would now happily chug along at a walking pace. Stub axle extensions gave an equivalent hike in ground clearance at the front. Extra underbody protection was provided in the form of guards for the sump and steering box, and a self-locking differential helped provide better traction when the going got sticky.

These improvements formed the basis

Kübelwagen (Type 82) 1940–5

Engine

Type	Air-cooled flat-four
Capacity	985cc/1,131cc
Max. power	23bhp/25bhp
Top speed	50mph (80km/h)

Transmission

Gearbox	Manual four-speed, with reduction gearing

Suspension

Front	Independent with transverse torsion bars and trailing arms
Rear	Independent with swing axles and torsion bars

Dimensions

Weight	1,585lb (720kg)

Kübelwagen Type 82 – a light, simple, but effective vehicle, the Kübelwagen saw service from the Sahara Desert to the Russian Steppes. Rommel loved it, and Allied troops were keen to use as many as they could capture.

for a Kübelwagen Mk2, the Type 82. The modifications made it some 100kg heavier than the Type 62, but at 750kg, it was still impressively lightweight for a military vehicle.

Still, not everyone was happy with the Kübelwagen. Opposition came from high within the Wehrmacht hierarchy. One argument was that with only 23bhp, the KdF-Wagen was underpowered. Another was that without four-wheel-drive the Kübel would become hopelessly bogged down when trying to cross wartime terrain. Defenders of the vehicle countered this by pointing out its excellent traction, thanks to the weight of the engine over the rear-driven wheels, and also that under the sort of conditions where even a four-wheel-drive

Doubts were cast on whether the low-powered Kübelwagen was up to military use. But as these shots show, it proved it could cope with harsh terrain – and, when it did get stuck, the Kübel was light enough to be man-handled back on course.

vehicle would founder, at least the light-weight Kübel could be pushed out by its two occupants and got going again. The gripes quickly disappeared when Hitler stepped in and gave the Kübelwagen his express backing, and production of the Kübelwagen began at Wolfsburg in February 1940.

As a military vehicle it proved an enor-mous success. More than 55,000 Kübels were made before the war ended, and they saw service from the Russian front to the Libyan Desert. Erwin Rommel had tried out the Kübel while taking part in the offensive across northern France, and he had been deeply impressed by it – so impressed, that when he took charge of the campaign in North Africa, he insisted that

Kübelwagen bodies were manufactured by Berlin military coachbuilder Ambi-Budd, then taken to Wolfsburg for final assembly. More than 55,000 Kübelwagens were made during the war.

a large number of his existing vehicles be replaced by Kübelwagens. Their air-cooled engines were less affected by air-borne dust than more conventional units, they proved able to soak up a tremendous amount of punishment, and when – as frequently occurred – a Kübel rolled over while traversing a sand dune, two men could easily push it upright again. Its traction in desert conditions was also remarkable. Rommel, it's said, quipped that in the desert a Kübelwagen could be driven where a camel could barely walk.

The German rank-and-file liked the Kübelwagen just as much as Rommel did, while captured examples proved popular with allied personnel. US soldiers were even issued with a booklet telling them how to use and maintain captured Kübels.

Not surprisingly, considering the vast range of duties the Kübel was asked to per-

A small number of KdF-Wagens, like this 1942 model, trickled out of the Wolfsburg factory during the war years.

form, Porsche was soon put to work designing variations adapted for specific military roles. There was a Kübelwagen fitted with flanged wheels so it could run on railway lines; one made specially for Rommel's Afrika Korps, featuring balloon tyres to cope with the Saharan sand; and another (which never made it into production) which had rear caterpillar tracks designed for the mud and snow of the Eastern Front.

One bizarre version, the Type 230, was built in response to the increasing shortage of fuel Germany experienced as World War Two wore on. With petroleum-based fuels

Wartime petrol shortages led to the development of the remarkable solid-fuel burning Kübelwagen (above) and KdF-Wagen (right). Simply tip coal, peat or wood into the generator under the front bonnet, light up and off you go.

Schwimmwagen – the Water Beetle

One of the more interesting developments on the military Beetle theme was the Schwimmwagen, or amphibious VW. This intriguing vehicle had a water-tight body and a propeller which gave it a speed of around 6mph (10km/h) in water.

A vehicle like this has clear advantages in military conditions: where conventional vehicles are held up when they reach a river, causing a bottleneck until a bridge can be built or repaired, the Schwimmwagen simply heads straight into the water, lowers its propeller and is across and ready to advance again in minutes. However, the high cost of constructing the Schwimmwagen meant that relatively few were built.

'Schwimmwagen' is a title that actually covers a number of aquatic Volkswagens. The earliest Type 128 had the Kübelwagen's extra ground clearance, plus four-wheel-drive and an extra-low gear ratio. Its body was a watertight tub welded from sheet steel, with rubber seals keeping the water from entering at the various apertures needed for drive shafts, steering column and so on. The engine was mounted in a separate waterproof compartment. This engine was the more powerful 1,131cc unit.

Once in the water a three-bladed propeller was lowered into position, connected to the engine by a simple dog clutch. The steering wheel continued to be used to alter direction – when turned, the front wheels acted like a boat's rudder, though not quite so efficiently.

The Schwimmwagen was one of the most versatile and effective wartime Volkswagens. As this action pic shows, it was as good at scaling cross-country obstacles as it was at crossing rivers.

The Type 128 had room for five soldiers and their kit, and sensibly carried a pair of paddles for use in emergencies.

From the 128 evolved the Type 138 in 1941, based on a backbone chassis. Later on there was a more compact version of the Schwimmwagen, the Type 166. This had a 40cm shorter wheelbase and weighed some 40kg less than the original Type 128.

Thanks to its four-wheel-drive the Type 166 was as much at home on the land as it was in the water, exhibiting outstanding cross-country ability. Porsche's son Ferry carried out much of the testing, using the car to scale several mountain peaks which had never before been reached by motor vehicles. Of one ascent, of the Kitzbüheler Horn, Ferry recalled in his memoirs 'the plateau on the summit is so small that we could not turn the car under its own power – we had to lift it by hand and turn it round to begin the descent'.

Its abilities were also recognized by the US Supreme Command who, after testing a captured Schwimmwagen, reported incredulously that it could do everything a US Jeep could do, used only half as much fuel, and it could swim as well!

Schwimmwagens were understandably in high demand from German forces during the war. Of the total of 14,283 made, most went to the elite units of the SS.

The Type 166 was a smaller, lighter and more agile version of the original Type 128 Schwimmwagen.

Schwimmwagen (Type 128) (1940–1)

Engine
Type	Air-cooled flat-four
Capacity	1,131cc
Max. power	25bhp
Top speed	50mph (80km/h) (land); 6mph (10km/h) (water)

Transmission
Gearbox	Manual four-speed + 4WD, with reduction gearing

Suspension
Front	Independent with transverse torsion bars and trailing arms
Rear	Independent with swing axles and torsion bars

Dimensions
Weight	1,985lb (900kg)

being restricted to high-priority uses such as the Luftwaffe and frontline vehicles, the Type 230 was designed to run on alternative fuels. Incorporating a bulbous gas generator stove in front of the windscreen, it could use whatever fuels were locally available, from wood chips to coal or even peat.

In early 1943, in a much delayed response to those original complaints that the Kübelwagen was underpowered, a larger engine was fitted. Boring out the cylinders increased the capacity of the air-cooled flat-four from its original 985cc to 1,131cc, and power increased from 23bhp to 25bhp.

A four-wheel-drive Kübelwagen prototype was also designed, but never made it into production. Its four-wheel-drive system did see service, however, on another Volkswagen called the Kommandeurwagen. This was basically a KdF-Wagen bodyshell mounted on a four-wheel-drive Kübelwagen chassis. Some 670 Komandeurwagens were built, most going to Rommel's Afrika Korps. They featured the full-length sliding fabric sunroof which had been originally presented as an option on the KdF-Wagen.

Another version, the Type 82E, was similar to the Kommandeurwagen, except that it was based on the standard two-wheel-drive Kübelwagen chassis. Due to the reduction gearing fitted to their rear hubs, these vehicles sat higher than the standard KdF-wagen, and are immediately recognizable by the extra space beneath their wheel arches.

Ferdinand Porsche undertook a number

The Kommandeurwagen was a tough, no-nonsense Beetle based on the raised Kübelwagen chassis with four-wheel-drive. It made ideal transport for high-ranking officers in frontline conditions.

The Maus *tank was a last-ditch terror weapon dreamt up by Hitler. Too heavy and cumbersome to be of practical use, Porsche agreed to build it against his better judgement. The soldier on the left seems to agree.*

of other commissions for military vehicles during the war. Most famous was his design for the Tiger tank, which featured twin air-cooled engines. One less successful prototype he was instructed to build towards the end of the war was the Mouse, an enormous tank that resembled a land-based battleship. It carried 25cm-thick armour plating, and – recalling Porsche's earliest hybrid designs – had a vast 1,500bhp Mercedes diesel engine powering electric generators which in turn fed twin electric motors driving the tracks.

It seems that the Mouse was meant to be one of Hitler's last-ditch terror weapons, designed to strike fear into the advancing allied troops. In practice, the Mouse was too big and cumbersome to be of practical use. The glaring problem was that if this fearsome 180-tonne tank ever got bogged down in the mud, there was nothing capable of ever pulling it out again.

Wartime production at the Volkswagen factory wasn't limited to military vehicles. Wolfsburg was also kept busy producing a range of armaments, including Junkers aircraft and the V1 'Doodlebug' flying bomb. To counter these weapons the Allies took the decision to target the factory for bombing raids. During 1944, bombers attacking in daylight destroyed two-thirds of the factory buildings and left 73 dead and 160 wounded.

From the autumn of 1944 onwards an increasing proportion of the production machinery was shut down and placed in storage. Despite this, by the end of the year the 12,000 workers (only a third of whom were German) had produced 20,884 vehicles. Total production of military Volkswagens of all types during the war years exceeded 66,000. In that time the Beetle's running gear had been put through the most rigorous testing and development exercise imaginable.

4 Order out of Chaos

One morning in May 1945 workers at the war-torn Volkswagen factory awoke to find that the storm troopers who had guarded them had disappeared. Many of these workers were prisoners from Poland and Russia who had been drafted in to work as slave labour at the factory. In comparison with conditions at other sites in Nazi Germany, the treatment of prisoners at Wolfsburg had not been excessively callous. Nonetheless, these prisoners had several years' worth of resentment to work off. Freed at last, they were out for retribution. Mobs formed, machinery was vandalized and blood was shed.

American forces had already passed very close to KdF-Stadt, but they had missed the town because it wasn't shown on their maps. So a deputation set out from the factory to find and meet them, with the aim of bringing them in to impose some order on the chaos prevailing there.

During his visits to America before the war, Ferdinand Porsche had persuaded a number of German engineers living in the US to return to Germany and help produce the Volkswagen. One of these engineers, a French friar and a German priest, made up the unlikely team that drove off to meet the advancing US troops – a risky undertaking in an unsettled countryside teeming with trigger-happy soldiers.

Fortunately, the threesome managed safely to contact troops from the 102nd US Infantry. At first they were shown little sympathy; US officers weren't too impressed when they learnt that Americans, even German-born Americans, had deserted the US to help the German war effort. But when it was pointed out that some of the children of the Germans who had returned from America still held official US citizenship, the response changed dramatically. US troops were diverted to the Volkswagen works and quickly imposed order on it.

The end of the war left the Volkswagen factory in a precarious situation. For a while it was marooned in an uneasy no-man's land between the Russians and the Americans. When the lines were drawn up for the partitioning of Germany among the Allied forces, it fell into the British sector – but only just. The East German border, with its watch towers and barbed wire, went up just 4km (2.5 miles) from the factory. It's interesting to speculate what the future might have held for the Beetle if fate had placed it in Russian, not British, hands. Maybe as a Soviet people's car, it would have enjoyed as much of a cult following in Vladivostok as it did in Los Angeles.

Not that the future looked anything like bright for the Volkswagen factory even though it was in British hands. War had severely disrupted German agricultural production, food was desperately short and there was a serious threat of famine and disease. The need to re-establish a basic infrastructure was paramount, and few people had time to spare to think about this battered factory, with its unpleasant Nazi connotations and its peculiar little beetle-backed cars.

More ominously still, those who did give some thought to the factory saw it as a useful source of war reparations, to be dismantled and distributed among the Allies in repayment for the terrific cost of the war. French Industry Minister, Marcel Paul, was keen to transport the production lines wholesale to France and manufacture Volkswagens there (France's own motor industrialists were predictably a lot less enthusiastic about this idea), and the Australian government also expressed an interest in the plant.

That the Volkswagen factory did survive, and began producing cars again, is thanks to a hefty dose of good luck – and to the remarkable foresight of the British army officers from REME – the Royal Electrical and Mechanical Engineers – whose job it was to oversee the site.

Although large parts of the factory lay in ruins, important machinery had survived and there was still a substantial German workforce who, although undernourished and dispirited, were keen to set to work and build themselves a new future. While pushing through occupied Europe, Allied forces had captured numerous German

---

Humber rejects the Beetle

The man who turned down The Beatles is often cited as the classic example of someone who misses out on the chance of a lifetime. This hapless music executive listened to one of The Beatles' early demo tapes and dismissed them as a bunch of no-hopers. Subsequently, of course, they went on to super stardom and he was left to rue his expensive mistake.

But if that was a disastrously missed sales opportunity, what of the man who turned down not the Beatles but the Beetle - the head of British car manufacturer Humber, Sir William Rootes? Rootes visited Wolfsburg in 1946 to investigate the Beetle, and dismissed it as an uneconomic proposition. If he hadn't, the British motor industry might be in very different shape today.

The full story is a little more complicated. As Ivan Hirst himself has pointed out, Rootes was never actually offered the chance to take over the Volkswagen plant. How could he have been, when in 1946 no one was even sure who owned the factory? On the other hand, because he didn't rate the Beetle's chances, Rootes would have had no reason to investigate whether Volkswagen was up for grabs. If he'd thought the Beetle was a potential best-seller (and a threat to his own future models) history might have taken a very different turn.

Humber's first encounter with Volkswagen occurred during the war, when the British company received a Type 82 Kübelwagen that had been captured at the Battle of El Alamein. Humber took it apart piece by piece (liberating large quantities of Saharan Desert in the process) and prepared a report for army intelligence. Although they conceded that 'the design is particularly interesting because it is quite uninfluenced by any previous traditions', their verdict clearly showed that they didn't rate the Kübel. 'Looking at the general picture, we do not consider that the design represents any special brilliance, apart from certain of the detail points, and it is suggested that it is not to be regarded as an example of first class modern design to be followed by the British industry.' This seems a surprising conclusion to reach, as the Kübelwagen had proved itself exceptionally fitted to its wartime role.

A government commission, headed by Sir William Rootes, which visited Wolfsburg in 1946 was even more damning. The factory, Rootes recommended, 'should be dismantled or it will collapse of its own inertia with two years'. Humber's engineers examined the Beetle and compared it with an experimental Hillman Minx. They praised the Beetle's body construction, with its extensive use of flanging (crimping two parts together) to reduce the amount of spot welding needed, but were distinctly unimpressed by the standard of finish of this early example. 'The car is painted entirely in Army Green and this is an exceedingly poor finish. No adequate measures seem to have been taken either for cleaning and de-greasing the stampings before priming, or any steps taken for rust-proofing, with the result that paintwork is peeling away from the vehicle.'

The engine also came in for criticism. Humber's engineers were surprised at its use of costly magnesium alloys, and called it noisy and rough.

In conclusion, Humber felt the vehicle 'does not meet the fundamental technical requirements of a motor car. As regards performance and design it is quite unattractive to the average motor car buyer. It is too ugly and too noisy. To build the car commercially would be a completely uneconomic enterprise'.

Oops! This verdict must have made bitter reading two decades later when, in the light of the Beetle's phenomenal sales success, the Rootes Group responded by launching its own rear-engined small car, the poorly built and ill-fated Hillman Imp.

But to be fair to Humber, it wasn't alone in its opinion of the Beetle. Henry Ford also came over from America to investigate buying Volkswagen – and reputedly thought it 'not worth a damn'. A number of factors put him off the Beetle. The close proximity of the East German border made the site politically unsettled, and then there was the problem of who actually owned Volkswagen. As a Nazi-run concern, the factory had been seized by the occupying Military Government, but whether ownership fell to them, the postwar German government, the State of Lower Saxony, the Trades Unions who claimed it was their money, sequestrated by the DAF, that had financed the factory, or even those thousands of citizens who had industriously filled in their Beetle savings cards, was a thorny question that wouldn't be settled for some time to come.

Above all the Beetle was too different a beast to the average American automobile – or, for that matter, the average British car. Even a decade after its design had first been sketched out, it still looked unnervingly futuristic. Whatever the engineering realities, the motor manufacturers of the day simply took one look at the Beetle, and decided the public would never swallow it. How wrong they were.

Not the world's clearest photograph, but it shows Henry Ford (centre) visiting Germany in 1948 to evaluate the Beetle. He decided it was 'not worth a damn', and, like Humber's Lord Rootes, declined to make a bid for the Wolfsburg works.

Allied bombing caused considerable damage at Wolfsburg during the last years of the war and left much of the production machinery in ruins. The British army's first job was to restore the basic infrastructure of the factory.

vehicles of all sorts. The British army's own light vehicles were in desperately short supply, so it made sense for REME to give the Volkswagen workers the task of repairing and maintaining these captured cars.

This work was overseen at first by Colonel Michael McEvoy. What McEvoy also quickly discovered was that all the supplies and key machinery needed to make the production of new vehicles a practical proposition already existed. The most obvious vehicle to put back into production for the Allied forces to use was the Kübelwagen. This, however, proved impossible, because the supplier of Kübelwagen bodies, Ambi-Budd, was located in East Berlin, now under Russian authority.

Surprisingly, some Kübelwagen bodyshells did arrive at the Volkswagen works after the war had ended, but as Russia tightened its control over its sector the supply dried up. However, some 138 Kübelwagens were assembled from the parts available in June 1945. Further Kübels were built in diminishing numbers over the following months as parts were gradually used up. In total 522

Kübelwagens were built in 1945.

That left the KdF-Wagen as the next obvious candidate for production. McEvoy, who had actually ridden in one of the pre-production KdF-Wagens at a Berlin motor show before the war, felt this would be an ideal vehicle for British forces to use in their occupation role. Best of all, it could be built at no cost to the British Treasury.

On a warm sunny day in August 1945, a pivotal figure in the Beetle's future arrived at the Volkswagen factory – Major Ivan Hirst. His first encounter with a Volkswagen had taken place one year before, when his army workshop in Normandy had taken apart a captured Kübelwagen. Hirst had been impressed by its advanced features.

He agreed with McEvoy's view that there should be an effort to put the Volkswagen works back into car production. He obtained a 1942 KdF-Wagen, sprayed it khaki green and demonstrated it before top brass at the British Military Government's headquarters. They were obviously impressed – Hirst returned with an order for 10,000 cars.

Ivan Hirst

Yorkshireman Ivan Hirst was a twenty-nine-year-old British Army major when he arrived at Wolfsburg in August 1945. Although his background was in optical engineering, he was by the end of the war well equipped to take on responsibility for the Volkswagen factory. He had run a tank repair workshop which followed the Allied advance across Europe, and he spoke good German. More importantly, he possessed qualities of compassion and understanding that enabled him quickly to get the German workers at Wolfsburg on his side. In those dismal days of depression, shortages and rock-bottom morale, this was every bit as difficult a task as rebuilding the physical fabric of the factory.

Hirst steered Volkswagen through its darkest days, when the threat of closure was imminent and few people outside the factory had any confidence in its long-term prospects. It was Hirst who recognized the qualities of Heinrich Nordhoff. Hirst interviewed Nordhoff for the post of deputy manager of the Wolfsburg factory, but was so impressed by Nordhoff's knowledge and experience that he decided to take him on as Director General instead. After Nordhoff took over, Hirst stayed at the factory in a background role, wanting to see the Volkswagen project through even though it meant turning down an attractive job offer from Ford.

Major Ivan Hirst, who took over at Wolfsburg in August 1945, ran the factory on enlightened principles. He restored the morale of a disheartened German workforce and, against all odds, set the Beetle on the road to success.

When Hirst did take his leave, Volkswagen tried to express their appreciation for what he had done by presenting him with a Beetle cabriolet. As a British officer, Hirst felt he couldn't accept such a generous gift, but he was pleased to receive a specially commissioned scale model of the Beetle, and this became a cherished possession.

Hirst continued working in Germany until national autonomy returned in the mid-1950s. Later he worked for the Organization for Economic Co-operation and Development in Paris, before retiring to his native Yorkshire. Fittingly, he was invited as an honoured guest to the twenty-millionth-Beetle celebrations held in Mexico in 1981.

One Volkswagen derivative built soon after the war was this post office delivery van.

This order set a clear direction for the factory. It was officially requisitioned for a four-year period, during which it would carry out essential work for the occupying forces. The threat that Wolfsburg might be closed down began to recede.

There was plenty of repair work needing urgent attention at the war-ravaged factory. Hirst called in sappers to repair the sewerage system, and set some farmland within the factory precincts back into production to provide much-needed food.

A change of image was needed too. A town called KdF-Stadt carried unacceptable connotations of the defeated Nazi regime, so it was decided to change the name to Wolfsburg after the nearby estate with its distinctive castle. The name Volkswagen was also tainted with the unhappy associations of its Nazi past, so Hirst suggested changing the factory name to Wolfsburg Motoren Werke – in the same

way that BMW stood for Bayerische Motoren Werke. Signposts were put up to this effect, but the name didn't catch on. 'Motor' in German means engine, and while this was fine for BMW, who had started out producing aero engines, it seemed a less suitable description for Volkswagen, a car manufacturer. Whatever stigma that did attach to the Volkswagen title soon faded away, and the name stuck.

Looking back at these events today, what stands out is the amazingly fore-sighted and compassionate behaviour of Hirst and his fellow officers in charge of the VW factory. This, remember, was after five years of bloody war, ending in a hard-fought struggle to liberate Europe that had been protracted by the refusal of the Nazi leadership to admit that they were beaten. Sympathy for the recently defeated enemy was in short supply, and there was more enthusiasm for making Germany atone for the damage it had caused than helping the country back onto its feet. America's Marshall Aid plan, which provided Germany with financial assistance, wouldn't be announced for a couple of years to come.

Yet Ivan Hirst recognized the important role Volkswagen could play in rebuilding the shattered German economy, and he steered the re-emerging car-making facility towards this goal. Not everyone was happy with this strategy. Some felt it made no sense for the British to actively rebuild a German motor industry that might one day take sales from Britain's car makers.

Hirst proved progressive too in his treatment of the Volkswagen work force. At the end of the war, when the Allies were actively pursuing a policy of 'denazification', gatherings of Germans were banned. Nevertheless, Hirst obtained permission for workers to elect their own Works Council, a co-operative organization which could make important decisions on working practices, including working hours and holiday allowances.

The employees, who numbered around 6,000 at this time, responded to Hirst's initiatives and worked enthusiastically under him to get the Volkswagen plant moving again. Life at Wolfsburg in the severe winter of 1946–47 was harsh. Workers put in long days – seven in the morning till six at night – and all that was usually available in the canteen at lunchtime was watery cabbage soup. At this time a pound of butter cost more than the average worker's monthly wage, and there were continuing shortages of food and clothing.

Despite the hardships, the production lines started moving again. By the end of 1945 a mixed bag of Volkswagens had been produced. As well as the 522 Kübelwagens made that year, the factory turned out a variety of vans and delivery vehicles, based on the Kübelwagen chassis. The first post-

war Beetles built were Type 51s, again based on the Kübelwagen chassis with its reduced gearing and raised ground clearance – 703 of these Type 51s were made before the year ended. In contrast, the standard Beetle saloon numbered only 58, making a total of 2,490 vehicles produced by the plant during 1945.

The British added their own contribution to the tortuous saga of Volkswagen type numbers. The Beetle saloon, which had started out as Porsche Type 60, then changed to VW Type 1 while it was known as the KdF-Wagen, now became VW Type 11. The second digit referred to a code number for the body style: '1' meant the two-door saloon body, whilst a Beetle fitted with a sliding sunroof was known as the Type 13.

Now that Ivan Hirst had established a demand among occupying forces for the standard Beetle saloon, production focused on this model, and 7,677 were turned out during 1946. Batches were prepared for the Russians (painted maroon), the RAF (blue), the French (light grey), and the Americans (dark grey).

In the early part of 1946, a further 102 Type 51s were built until the stocks of Kübelwagen parts were exhausted – a solitary Kübelwagen was also built, plus a handful of trailers. Overall production for 1946 totalled 7,787, and on 14 October the 10,000th postwar VW rolled off the production lines.

Considering the difficulties and hardships of the time, this was no mean achievement. And although working conditions remained poor – a shortage of coal halted production during early 1947 – the following year saw another 8,987 Beetles produced.

Not surprisingly, these early cars had their faults. Paintwork quality was crude, oil coolers leaked and some engines needed an overhaul before they'd covered 20,000

Ivan Hirst takes the wheel of the 1,000th Beetle to come off the reactivated Wolfsburg production line – no mean achievement in those days of hunger, shortages and a demoralized workforce.

miles. Parts shortages meant that many cars had to make do with a single front windscreen wiper, whilst there was also a problem caused by the odour of the adhesive used to fix interior trim into place – it was a fish-based glue, and when it got damp in wet weather it let off an awful stench.

It took a while to get some components up to acceptable standards. The front shock absorbers were very weak, which gave these very early cars an alarming tendency to tip over if cornered hard. More seriously, a number of accidents occurred, some fatal. Faulty steering was identified as the cause, and it emerged that the steer-

ing arms, which were made in a separate factory at Hagen, were being forged from flawed steel ingots.

REME personnel investigated all these defects, and made whatever modifications were necessary. Because of the shortages at the time, these were often minimalist: the cacophonous engine noise of early models, for instance, was combated simply by placing stiff cardboard in the engine bay.

Despite its faults, there was considerable enthusiasm for the Beetle from Germans and British alike. Major Charles Bryce (the REME officer in charge of Inspection at Wolfsburg in 1946) later recalled:

Radclyffe roadster – the original 'rag-top' Beetle

In the immediate postwar years the struggle for survival of the ravaged Volkswagen factory left little time for research and development. But the British officers governing Wolfsburg did find time to develop one intriguing variation on the Volkswagen theme – an open-top two-seater based on the Beetle. What became known as the Radclyffe roadster was an interesting little car in its own right, but what makes it doubly significant is that it certainly provided the inspiration for the official Beetle two-seater cabriolet made by Hebmüller.

The idea for the Radclyffe roadster came indirectly from Colonel Michael McEvoy, who at that time was responsible for overseeing the running of vehicle maintenance workshops throughout Germany. McEvoy had connections with the motor industry going back before the war. Among other accomplishments, he had produced specials based on British cars, acquired UK rights to Zoller superchargers, and worked as a consultant for Daimler-Benz.

Like Porsche before him, McEvoy wanted to build a racing Volkswagen. He discussed the idea with an old Mercedes-Benz friend, Rudy Uhlenhaut, who had been responsible for designing the Mercedes Grand Prix racers of the 1930s. Uhlenhaut came up with some sketches that involved making drastic modifications to the Beetle, turning its engine and transmission round so it effectively became a mid-engined car.

McEvoy took these sketches to Hirst, who being up to his eyeballs in the day-to-day running of the plant, didn't share his friend's enthusiasm. But it set the idea growing in Hirst's mind that a more sporty version of the Beetle might broaden its sales potential. Consequently, he gave the tiny experimental workshop at the factory the task of designing a prototype convertible.

They came up with a disarmingly simple design. Tooling up for a new engine cover would have been far too costly, so they circumvented this problem by altering a front bonnet and fitting it to the rear of the car.

This prototype was finished off by (hence its name) Col. Charles Radclyffe, who was in control of light engineering in the British zone. Radclyffe used the car with enthusiasm throughout the

The Radclyffe roadster was a cheap and cheerful open-top Beetle – to save money, the engine lid panel was simply a relocated bonnet. Only one of these was built, but it provided inspiration for the pretty Hebmülller Cabriolet.

summer of 1947, though it had to be given a new engine and chassis after a collision with a steel bar on the autobahn wiped out the underside of the car. Apparently twin carburettors were fitted to the engine, giving extra power, but also a bad case of flat-spotting.

The Radclyffe roadster was a common sight at Wolfsburg throughout 1947, at a time when representatives of coachbuilding company Hebmüller paid frequent visits to the site. Probably no coincidence, then, that when the elegant, but sadly short-lived, Hebmüller Cabriolet appeared a couple of years later, it bore a striking family resemblance to Wolfsburg's own Radclyffe roadster.

There was something special about the Beetle that aroused the utmost enthusiasm in all who had anything to do with it, and with all its defects and troubles in 1946 this fever existed among us all. I can offer no logical explanation for this – after all, it was quite an ugly looking little beast, performance was not so wonderful and, in 1946, it was crudely finished. Yet we were just as VW daft then as are so many modern Beetle owners.

In spite of its problems, the Volkswagen factory now had a clear future. The threat that machinery might be dismantled for war reparations had faded away, and as the first signs of recovery appeared in Germany it was obvious that a large domestic market for motor cars would one day emerge. By the end of 1947 the market for the Beetle had already expanded considerably. Although initially allowed to sell only to the occupying bodies, Ivan Hirst soon obtained permission to sell cars to British officers at a price of £160 each. Then, at the 1947 Hanover Fair, the Beetle was officially launched and offered for sale to the general public – although at that time, few people in Germany were in a position to afford one.

EXPORTS

A number of Beetles began quietly finding their way out of Germany. One of these was responsible for starting an early unofficial export business to England. The car was bought as a part-exchange deal by Surrey car dealer John Colborne-Baber; speaking in the early 1970s, he recalled:

In 1948 a Swedish gentleman returned from Germany driving a one-year-old Volkswagen. He had bought himself a farm in Cornwall and said the Volkswagen was not going to be much use to him there. He noticed I had a Buick station wagon for sale and was interested in doing a deal. I rang up various friends in the trade and asked them if they knew what a VW was worth. No one knew a thing about it. I eventually bought it for £150 against the Buick, with a little trepidation as I had sold a certain quantity for what seemed to me at the time to be a very uncertain one.

After running the VW for ten days, I decided that it was streets ahead of anything I had driven in the small car class. Its gearbox and gear-ratios were absolutely right. It was rather like driving a little 3-litre Bentley – the axle ratio was 3.5:1, exactly the same, and the gear ratios very nearly the same, so you got that sort of impression. It was a little saloon car that you could drive as a sports car, and don't forget the only cars we had to compare it with were things like the Austin 8 and the Standard 8, which were both ghastly vehicles.

I announced to the staff that we were going to specialize in the Volkswagen

John Colborne-Baber, the first motor dealer to sell Beetles in Britain.

because I thought it was a car that would go all over the world.

At this time importing new cars for sale in the UK wasn't permitted. However, Colborne-Baber began buying up the spare parts packs that came with each Beetle, and accumulating them in the storeroom at his garage in Ripley, Surrey. Wherever possible he would also buy the cars that had been brought in as personal imports, refurbish them and sell them on.

> We found that the Volkswagens weren't acceptable to the British public in their normal state, with their sack-cloth upholstery and their rather bad paintwork. So we used to re-upholster them in leather, in preference to imitation leather cloth, because there was purchase tax on leather cloth then, but no tax on leather, which meant the latter was cheaper! We then repainted them, removing the engine, windows and wings and fitting new rubbers and piping. We used to say any colour you like, so if they wanted it upholstered in red and painted pink they could have it.

These Beetles were made even more attractive by the addition of chromed brightwork to the body, hubcaps and bumpers, and a conversion to right-hand-drive was also offered. Around one hundred of these reconditioned Colborne-Baber cars were sold over a four-year period, the company at one stage having a waiting list of sixty customers. Prices in 1951 were £410, or £425 if a right-hand-drive conversion was specified. The original car, bought in part-exchange for the Buick, returned to the family when John Colborne-Baber's son, Peter, spotted it on the forecourt one day in the mid-1970s, and snapped it up from its surprised owner, who had only called in to buy some spares.

Meanwhile, back at Wolfsburg official exports of the Beetle were beginning to Dutch dealer Ben Pon. He had been interested in securing import rights for the Volkswagen in the days before the war broke out, and when production began again he reopened his enquiries. In August 1947 he was designated official VW importer for the Netherlands, and received his first batch of 56 cars. Unlike the cars

The original Colborne-Baber Beetle. Between 1947 and 1951 John Colborne-Baber obtained around 100 Beetles that had been imported to the UK by returning servicemen. He gave them a distinctive facelift and then put them on sale to the public.

available in Germany, these had a slightly better specification which included chromed bumpers and hubcaps.

Interestingly, Pon's first delivery was held up on Ivan Hirst's orders until sufficient spares had been assembled to accompany them. Hirst had personal experience of fleets of trucks disabled during the war due to lack of spare parts, and was determined that this wouldn't happen to the Beetle. So began the strict Volkswagen rule never to export Beetles without making sure an adequate batch of spares accompanied them – a rule that helped the compa-

Colborne-Baber's Beetles featured leather interiors and chromed brightwork, hubcaps and bumpers; even the engine was treated to a chromed inlet manifold and pulley wheel.

The first batch of Beetles to be officially exported line up in 1947 ready to go to the Netherlands.

ny keep customers loyal in difficult export markets over the years to come.

With sales expanding in all these directions, Ivan Hirst realized it was time to bring in a motor industry professional who possessed the necessary experience to build on Volkswagen's shaky postwar renewal and transform the company into a serious car producer. That man was Heinrich Nordhoff, and he was destined to play a central role in the Beetle's development over the next twenty years.

Hirst's original thought was to offer Nordhoff the job of deputy manager at the plant. But after meeting him, Hirst was so impressed by the German's practical knowledge of the motor industry that he decided he would make an ideal general manager. Although Nordhoff had experienced some hardship since the end of the

war, he didn't immediately jump at this opportunity. Like many others in the German motor industry, he'd watched the development of the people's car project under Hitler's patronage with a degree of cynicism. He'd regarded it as a political stunt, which gave birth to a pampered progeny that would never survive if it was forced to fend for itself in the competitive world. When Nordhoff had a good look at the Beetles being produced in 1947, he didn't find much reason to change his mind. Speaking in 1954, he said:

In January 1948, when I took over the management of the Volkswagen factory, I regarded the Volkswagen with the utmost scepticism. It was tarred with the brush of political trickery, and, the way it looked at the time, it was anything but a beauty.

It was badly painted, badly sprung,

Heinrich Nordhoff

Heinrich Nordhoff, who more than anyone else was the architect of the Beetle's postwar success, was born in Hildesheim on 6 January 1899. He graduated from the Berlin Charlottenburg technical university in 1927 and started his career as an apprentice with BMW. Nordhoff moved to Opel at Russelsheim, where he began to show his ability, moving steadily up the company hierarchy. Work was Nordhoff's passion, and it brought out his competitive spirit. Working at Opel, he later revealed, seemed to him 'more like a sport, in which one wants to show off one's ability'.

Opel was owned in the 1930s by US giant General Motors, and Nordhoff visited America to study mass production techniques. By the time war arrived Nordhoff had made it to board level, being appointed managing director of Opel's lorry division at Brandenburg – the biggest truck plant in Europe. When the war was over this factory fell in the US sector, which caused Nordhoff great difficulties. He had been awarded honours by the Nazi regime, and the Americans had a strict policy of not giving important jobs to anyone tainted with a hint of Nazism. They were moreover still angry that an American-funded plant had been used to make military vehicles. There was clearly no future for Nordhoff in the American sector, and for a couple of years he had trouble making ends meet.

Fortunately for him, British regulations did not prohibit him from taking up a position in their sector. Nordhoff was approaching fifty years of age when he accepted the job of Direktor-General

The man behind the Beetle's extraordinary postwar success, Heinrich Nordhoff. Beetle output rose under Nordhoff's stewardship from under 20,000 in 1948 to over 1.1 million in 1968, the year of his death. However, Nordhoff's uncompromising methods won him criticism as well as praise.

at Wolfsburg. It was a more difficult decision than it might seem, because like many others at the time, Nordhoff harboured grave reservations about the future of the Volkswagen.

Nordhoff hadn't even driven a Beetle when he took on the job. When he did, he began to form a new opinion about its chance of success. After his first drive he exclaimed 'This is no common or garden motor car. This car is something out of the ordinary, it has personality!'

As far as personalities went, Nordhoff stamped his own strong character on Wolfsburg. He ruled the factory as a patriarch, unhappy to accept criticism but sensitive to the lot of his workers. The door of his office was open to anyone, and in 1954 he commented:

> The value of an industrial organization is not made up by buildings and machines, not by capital and bank accounts, but by the spirit in which the thousands of people who work in it approach their duties. You can build factories as big and impressive as you like, as long as you have the money. But you cannot buy the spirit of an organization for all the money in the world – you have to create it yourself.

With boundless determination and energy, Nordhoff stuck to his aim of polishing the rough diamond that Ferdinand Porsche had bequeathed him, and in doing so he also achieved his goal of building the Volkswagen company into a major player in the German economy. In August 1955, on the occasion of the production of the millionth Beetle, Nordhoff was awarded the Grand Order of Merit with Star, the highest distinction of the German Republic.

Although the Beetle made him many friends, Nordhoff's uncompromising style made him enemies as well. His innate conservatism made him reluctant to diversify, with the result that VW became too heavily dependent on the Beetle. He frequently clashed with media and government, impatiently rejecting their advice. The stress told in stomach ulcers which needed surgery in 1958, and a serious heart attack he suffered in 1967.

By now control of VW was beginning to slip from Nordhoff's grasp. He was denied the chance to elect his successor, and was offered the position of honorary chairman, which would have left him with no real control over the company he had run for so long. But, before he had to decide whether to accept the indignity of taking up this offer, he suffered a fatal heart attack and died, aged sixty-nine, on 12 April 1968.

Early postwar Beetles, like this 1948 example, were still very basic, though specification varied from car to car. This one, for instance, boasts chromed bumpers and hubcaps which were not standard equipment at the time.

An historic moment – Col Radclyffe signs the agreement which passed control of the Wolfsburg factory back into German hands in September 1949. Nordhoff had already been running the plant for over a year under British supervision.

with mediocre brakes, a mediocre transmission, badly equipped and upholstered, noisy and hard-riding. But above all, its engine had absolutely no durability – overall it was a pretty miserable duckling!

But its designer, Professor Porsche, had worked something into it which made this rough diamond very much worth our while to polish.

Nordhoff accepted the job, and immediately set about working on the 'rough diamond' with exhausting vigour.

5 Beetle Conquers the World

Nordhoff took charge at the Volkswagenwerk on 1 January 1948. Officially, the plant remained under British control until September the following year, but when Nordhoff took on the job he insisted that he should be left to get on with it without anyone peering over his shoulder. 'The future', he declared portentously, 'begins only when all ties with the past have been severed.'

From the start, Nordhoff stamped his own distinctive style of management on the plant. His aim, he stated, was to build Volkswagen into 'a decisive factor in the German peacetime economy', and he achieved this ambition magnificently. Under his tutelage, the Beetle grew into a success story that the world of motoring will probably never match.

In those early days Volkswagen stood on the edge of a booming domestic market. The after-effects of the war, which had shattered the German economy and left the country poverty stricken, were beginning to recede. Things really looked up in June 1948 when the discredited Reichsmark was replaced by the Deutschmark. Goods started to reappear in the shops. Job opportunities opened up and the German people began to acquire the means – and the desire – to buy cars for themselves. Production at Wolfsburg more than doubled to 19,244 in 1948, and again to 46,146 the following year.

Germany desperately needed foreign currency, and Nordhoff knew that if Volkswagen was going to grow it had to export, but the Beetle at this time was still a depressingly austere vehicle. The car lacked any brightwork, with its dingy paintwork extending to cover bumpers, hubcaps and door handles. The interior was spartan, with no concessions to comfort or style, and soundproofing was rudimentary.

Nordhoff realized that in this form the Beetle didn't have a hope of attracting overseas buyers. What was needed was a separate model with a considerably higher standard of trim and specification. This, the Export or Deluxe model, he launched in July 1949.

The Export model boasted attractive gloss paintwork, alloy trim, and chrome-plated hubcaps, bumpers and door handles. Inside, it looked much plusher, with smart cloth upholstery, an attractive two-spoke steering wheel and a bright dashboard. These simple improvements transformed the look of the Beetle and set it up as a serious contender in export markets.

CABRIOLETS FROM KARMANN AND HEBMÜLLER

Around the same time as the Export model became available, an extra touch of glamour was added to the Beetle range with the introduction of a brace of cabriolets – a

Launched in 1949, the Export model marked a major step forward for the Beetle. Its attractive finish, with glossy paintwork, plenty of brightwork and a more comfortable interior, was designed to help it sell overseas.

two-seater by Hebmüller, and a five-seater from Karmann.

An open-top Beetle had always been part of the people's car agenda, and Adolf Hitler had even taken a ride in one at the inauguration of the Wolfsburg plant. But full development of this cabriolet was prevented by the outbreak of war. Afterwards, an open-top model seemed to be a natural addition to the Beetle range, hence Ivan Hirst's decision to give the experimental workshop at VW the task of designing what became the Radclyffe roadster.

There were others who shared Hirst's view. Germany had a long and proud tradition of coachbuilding. Many coachbuilding concerns could trace their origins back to the previous century, when they had made their living by fabricating ornate bodies for the horsedrawn carriages of the time. With the advent of the motor car, those who survived did so by adapting their skills to making bodywork that could be fitted to a rolling chassis provided by motor manufacturers.

War put an end to this. Many coachbuilding factories were adapted to produce armaments, and once the war was over they turned to making whatever basic goods they could simply to survive. But, by 1946, these coachbuilders were looking for ways to get back to their original trade. Hebmüller and Karmann both saw the potential of the newly reborn Beetle as the basis for coachbuilt designs.

Both companies were given permission to produce prototype open-top Beetles, being told to retain the existing running gear and as many existing saloon parts as possible to keep the production costs of the resulting models at a realistic level. Both prototypes were a success, and ultimately entered production as official open-top Volkswagen models.

Hebmüller Cabriolet

Hebmüller was founded in 1889, specializing in building horse-drawn carriages. After the death of the founder, Joseph, his four sons gave the firm a change in direction and began modifying car bodies. When World War Two ended, they were asked by the British Occupation Forces to build fifteen special-bodied cabriolets based on Humber chassis. These were a success, and soon afterwards came the commission from Wolfsburg for a two-seater cabriolet.

Hebmüller produced three prototypes, which had long curved engine covers reminiscent of the Radclyffe roadster. However, the 'Heb's' bootlid, unlike that of the Radclyffe car, wasn't a reworked bonnet, but an entirely new hand-crafted panel. With hoods that folded away out of sight

behind the seats, these prototypes possessed elegant, uncluttered lines. They also had a couple of major design flaws.

The first problem was that the bodyshells flexed badly. Unlike most of the cars the Hebmüller brothers had been used to working with, the Beetle didn't take all its strength from its chassis – the bodywork also played a part in the car's overall rigidity. Chop the roof off, and this rigidity was severely compromised. After a short drive over a rough road the body would be so badly warped that its doors couldn't close.

Hebmüller overcame this difficulty by adding a considerable amount of reinforcement. A pair of long, heavy, metal box-sections were welded under the sills, the front bulkhead gained a pair of strengthening plates, a hefty cross member was fixed below the rear occasional seat and several extra metal plates were welded into the inner panels at the rear of the car.

A second problem was that the standard rounded windscreen surround was too weak to take the tension when the hood was clipped into place. A reinforced square-edged windscreen was the answer.

A test car was built incorporating these modifications, and this proved to be quite rigid enough. It was driven hard over 6,000 miles (9,600km), many of them very rough, and stood up to the ordeal with no problems. Wolfsburg approved the design and assigned it Type number 14A. An order was placed for 2,000 cars, and production began in June 1949.

These production cars were kitted out with the full Deluxe specification, as well as their own special paintwork. Two-tone colour-schemes seemed to suit the 'Heb' particularly well, and the combinations on offer included black and ivory, black and red, black and yellow and red and ivory.

Even though it was quite a bit more

Hebmüller's sadly short-lived interpretation of the Beetle Cabriolet theme was a rather more elegant design than Karmann's. It was less spacious than its rival, though: rear accommodation was limited by the hood, which folds away neatly out of sight behind the seats.

expensive than the standard model, at DM7,500 (compared with DM5,450 for the Deluxe and DM4,850 for the standard saloon), the Hebmüller started selling well. Unfortunately, its success was short-lived. On 23 July 1949, a fire broke out at the Hebmüller works, destroying the paint-spraying facility and causing extensive damage elsewhere.

A massive clear-up operation began, and production restarted four weeks later. At first it seemed that this episode had been no more than a temporary blip in the company's progress. Production rates soon recovered – twenty-four Cabriolets were made in August, and January 1950 was the best month so far, with no fewer than 125 leaving the plant. But it soon became apparent that the fire had caused serious financial problems, which may have been

exacerbated by bad management. Production ground to a halt by the middle of 1950, and by 1952 Hebmüller had been registered bankrupt.

Ironically, the remaining bodies were taken to competitor Karmann for assembly. Around fifteen were made there, and the final car in a series that numbered around 750 (the exact total is uncertain) was built in February 1953. The Type 14A was then dropped, and the Karmann Cabriolet continued as the sole open-top Beetle.

Karmann Cabriolet

Karmann had been founded fifteen years before Hebmüller, in 1874, and switched from carriage to motor car body building early on after being given a commission by Dürkopp in 1902. Karmann struck up a

As well as a cabriolet, Hebmüller made this one-off Beetle coupé. Sadly, it no longer exists.

long-running relationship with successful motor manufacturer Adler, and by the time World War Two broke out, the Osnabrück-based coachbuilder was employing 600 people.

War brought a reversal of fortunes. The Karmann works was heavily bombed, and at the end of hostilities the company scraped by manufacturing unglamorous, but much needed, household goods. Wilhelm Karmann saw the revitalized Volkswagen as his chance to get back into coachbuilding. Being a German citizen, at this time he would have needed an official permit to be able to buy a Beetle, but he made approaches to the factory and, in November 1946, was given at no cost the 10,000th car produced to use as a guinea pig for a prototype cabriolet.

Like Hebmüller, Karmann encountered the problem of body flexing once they had removed the roof from the saloon. This was solved by the addition of reinforcements, which added 40kg to the car's weight. The saloon-style windscreen surround also needed replacing with a stronger squared-off item.

Because of its five-seater configuration, it was impossible for the Karmann Cabriolet to stow its hood neatly away as the Hebmüller could. It had to rest the furled hood back against the rear bodywork. This had the disadvantage of blanking off the row of engine cooling vents, and additional vents had to be cut into the engine cover to compensate. Even so, the Cabriolet engine was always less efficiently cooled than that of the saloon.

The first prototype had winding side windows at the front only, but this feature was extended to the rear side windows on a second prototype, which featured refinements such as a rear glass window in the hood, and concealed hood hinges.

Although these prototypes proved a success, shortages of material in those impoverished postwar days meant that further development had to take a back seat. It wasn't until the spring of 1949 that Volkswagen took twenty-five Cabriolets from Karmann and tested them over 12,000 miles. They came through with flying colours, and VW placed an initial order for 2,000. The model was officially dubbed the Type 15, and production began in September 1949.

Like the Hebmüller, the Karmann Cabriolet came equipped with the Deluxe trim level, and was available with a choice of two-tone paintwork – black and white, dark and light green, and brown and beige. It also carried the same DM7,500 price tag, which represented a considerable price premium over the saloon.

Despite the extra cost, the Karmann cabriolet wasn't short of buyers. By 1952 Karmann had made 10,000 cabriolets and were turning them out at the rate of 100 per day. The model sold strongly in export markets, and ultimately developed a particularly strong following in California. In time it became the world's most popular cabriolet (although it's now been eclipsed, fittingly enough, by the Golf Cabriolet),

Karmann's Cabriolet was designed to retain the Beetle's full five-seater capability – when not in use the hood folds back above the engine cover. Both front and rear windows can be wound down.

with a total of over 330,000 produced.

EXPORT DRIVE

Saloon and cabriolet, standard and deluxe. These models made up the Beetle range – all Nordhoff now had to do was sell them. At home in Germany, this task was eased by the expanding market that came with recovery after the war. Car-hungry Germans queued up to buy the Beetle, which in 1948 took almost two-thirds of the market share in Germany.

But in these early days this home market was still a volatile one, and it would have been risky for Nordhoff to rely on it. Full recovery was still a long way away. The Volkswagen had been designed as a people's car, but at the start of the 1950s the average German worker had to work 2,500 hours to be able to afford a Beetle – as opposed to 450 hours for his counterpart in the United States.

'Unless the Volkswagenwerk can tap a new reservoir of popular demand', argued the *Economist* at the time, 'it must push further into competitive markets overseas'. Heinrich Nordhoff fully agreed, and he embarked on a determined export drive. Exports expanded to Denmark, Luxembourg, Sweden, Switzerland and Belgium in 1948. In total 4,464 Beetles were sold abroad that year – which represented 23 per cent of production, and brought in DM21m of foreign currency.

Beetle production increased rapidly year on year through the 1950s, from 81,979 in 1950 to 279,986 in 1955 – the year that the millionth Beetle was built. Of this million, 400,000 had been exported to a staggering 103 countries. Waiting lists began to appear around the globe. Volkswagen's main difficulty appeared to be in producing enough cars quickly enough, and their marketing department translated its slogan 'Es lohnt sich, auf einen Volkswagen zu warten' (It's worth waiting for a Volkswagen) into just about every language.

Britain's *Motor* magazine was moved to

Endless train loads of Beetles left Wolfsburg bound for over 140 countries as sales soared in the 1950s.

Karmann Ghia – a touch of glamour

One car made a spectacular exception to Nordhoff's one-model rule in the 1950s. This was the Karmann Ghia, a delectable Italian-styled coupé built on Beetle running gear.

As a well-established coachbuilding company that already had the Beetle cabriolet to its credit, Karmann was in a strong position to put forward the idea of a sports model based on the Beetle. Its chief, Wilhelm Karmann, keenly wanted his company to build a distinct model in its own right. He put the idea to Heinrich Nordhoff several times in the early 1950s, but the latter gave discouraging replies. By now Nordhoff had determined that the way ahead lay in developing and refining the Beetle. He wasn't convinced that the still fragile German economy was ready for an expensive sports model, and he was reluctant to do anything that would divert resources from promoting the increasingly successful Beetle.

So the Karmann Ghia might never have seen the light of day, had it not been for the second half of the equation – Luigi Serge, commercial director of Italian styling house Carrozzeria Ghia. Wilhelm Karmann had discussed informally with him the possibility of Ghia building a prototype sports car based on the Beetle, and then showing it to Nordhoff to persuade him to give it the go-ahead.

Serge must have taken the idea to heart, because he had a prototype designed and made up, keeping its existence a secret not only from Nordhoff (who would certainly have vetoed it at this stage), but also from Karmann himself. The first Karmann knew of the car was when Serge invited him to see the completed prototype. Karmann had an extra surprise, because the car was not the convertible he had in mind, but a closed coupé.

He was not, however, disappointed. The prototype's elegant, flowing lines were in the finest traditions of Italian styling. Few hints were given that the engine was in the back, not under the front bonnet, and the complex design featured pillarless doors and curved window panes. It was a genuine piece of automotive art.

The next step was the tricky one – getting Nordhoff's approval. With much trepidation, Karmann invited Nordhoff to view the prototype in November 1953. Like Karmann, Nordhoff had no reservations about the car's styling. He did, however, think that it would be too costly to produce. Karmann argued that this shouldn't be a concern – he'd take all the production details out of Volkswagen's hands, by receiving rolling chassis direct from Wolfsburg, fitting the coupé bodywork, and only then returning the car to be sold at Volkswagen dealers alongside the Beetle. With surprising speed Nordhoff was talked round. Maybe even at this early stage he was anticipating the demands that were to come for additions to the Volkswagen range – or perhaps he simply fell for the coupé's styling. In any event, he gave his authority for it to go into production.

There was a small amount of fine-tuning to do first. The Beetle floorpan needed to be extended by 8cm on either side to accommodate the wider coupé bodywork. The steering column had to be angled downwards, and the gear lever shortened to match the coupé's lower seating position. Mechanically, of course, the car was Beetle through and through – it shared the Beetle's 1,192cc flat-four engine, transmission, brakes and suspension.

Building the car's curvaceous bodywork proved to be a labour-intensive job, drawing on all the skills of Karmann's craftsmen. The nose panel alone required five separate panels to be welded in place, the joints between them being painstakingly filled with lead. The wings were welded to the body, and then the whole assembly was bolted securely to the chassis.

Launch day was planned to be in August 1955, but it had to be brought forward to 14 July simply because Karmann lacked space in its tiny factory to store cars over that period. Almost as an afterthought, Karmann came up with a name for the coupé. In recognition of his and Ghia's imputs, it was to be officially called the Volkswagen Karmann Ghia. Its price was fixed at DM7,500, not an outlandish sum for a sports coupé in those days, but considerably more than the DM3,790 Beetle on which it was based.

A surprisingly frivolous diversion for VW came in 1955 with the launch of the delectable Karmann Ghia coupé. Although it was expensive, and more show than go, the Karmann Ghia proved to be an enduring success. A cabriolet version was launched in 1957.

The Karmann Ghia was well-received, but with one reservation. All were captivated by its looks, but many felt its performance left something to be desired. A 30bhp 1,192cc engine was fine for a budget saloon, but it felt feeble in a sleek sports design that promised something far more potent under the skin. That typical flat-four burble, so much a part of the Beetle's character, also seemed incongruous coming from this paragon of high fashion.

Soon, however, the Karmann Ghia established a market among those who wanted sporting style, but not necessarily sporting performance. The Karmann Ghia received all the engine and suspension updates that were made to the Beetle over the years, and this went some way to mollifying sportier drivers. All Karmann Ghia fans were overjoyed in late 1957 when a long-anticipated 'rag-top' version was revealed at the Frankfurt Show.

Extra body stiffening made the convertible slightly heavier, and hence slower, than the coupé, and at DM8,250 it was more expensive, too. But its glamorous sense of style won it many friends, particularly in America.

One brief sideshoot of the Karmann Ghia's development was the Type 34 Karmann Ghia, based on the Type 3 1500, which sold alongside the Beetle. Again styled by Ghia, this was a much less fluent piece of design, with sharp lines and an aggressive front end. It earned the nickname 'Razor-Edge'.

The much-anticipated open-top version of the Karmann Ghia appeared in 1957. Stylish it certainly was, but thanks to a price tag on a par with the MGA Twin-Cam and Austin Healey 3000, sales were never high.

No convertible version was made of the Razor-Edge, which sold in small numbers and was finally dropped in 1969. The Type 1 Karmann Ghia, meanwhile, having gained the 1,584cc, 50bhp engine from the 1302S Beetle in 1970, clung to life almost as tenaciously as its Beetle cousin. Production didn't come to an end at Karmann's Osnabrück factory until June 1974, when the much more up-to-date (if less good-looking) Scirocco replacement came on stream. The last batch headed west for America, where the Karmann Ghia had always met with particular affection.

comment in 1953 that Beetle output 'has risen with such remarkable rapidity that it has already become the People's Car of some other nations besides Germany'. In Switzerland, for instance, twenty-three per cent of all new cars bought in 1953 were Beetles.

As well as exporting fully built Beetles, Volkswagen sent them overseas in the form of Completely Knocked Down (CKD) kits. The first CKD kit was assembled by Irish Motor Distributors Ltd of Dublin in 1950. Among the numerous other CKD destina-

tions were Malaysia, New Zealand and Peru, while Australia, South Africa, Brazil and Mexico took the Beetle so much to heart that separate manufacturing plants were established in each of these countries.

Not all overseas markets proved so susceptible to the Beetle's charms. Britain – although it ultimately became VW's fourth largest market after America, Germany and Brazil – was at first slow to take to the Beetle. To some extent this was due to the anti-German feeling that lingered after the end of the war. Many people were reluctant

Karmann Ghia

Production totals	Type 1 (1955–74)	Type 3 (1962–69)
coupé	363,401	42,498
convertible	80,899	

Engine

Type	Air-cooled flat-four	Air-cooled flat-four
Capacity	1,192cc	1,493cc
Bore × stroke	77mm × 64mm	83mm × 69mm
Compression ratio	6.6:1	7.8:1
Max. power	30bhp @ 3,400rpm	45bhp @ 3,8000rpm
Max. torque	56lb/ft @ 2,000rpm	78lb/ft @ 2,000rpm

Transmission

Gearbox	Manual four-speed, with synchro on second, third and fourth	Manual four-speed, all synchromesh

Suspension

Front	Independent with transverse torsion bars and trailing arms, anti-roll bar	Independent with transverse torsion bars and trailing arms, anti-roll bar
Rear	Independent with swing axles, transverse torsion bars and trailing arms	Independent with swing axles, transverse torsion bars and trailing arms

Brakes

	Drum all-round	Drum all-round

Dimensions (in/mm)

Length	163/4,140	168/4,280
Width	64/1,630	64/1,620mm
Weight	1,760b (799kg)	1,755lb (796kg)

Performance

0–60mph	29sec	20sec
Top speed	76mph (121km/h)	66mph (105km/h)
Fuel consumption	34mpg (8.3l/100km)	31mpg (9.1l/100km)

Beetle production outside Germany

From its origins in Germany the Beetle became very much a world car, being exported to over 140 countries and actually being made in factories in some twenty countries. These are the countries where Beetles have been made, either in assembly plants for CKD kits, or in actual manufacturing plants. At one time or another manufacturing plants were running in Belgium, South Africa and Australia, as well, of course as Mexico and Brazil where production still continues.

Country	Production dates
Ireland	1951–1957
South Africa	1951–1979
Brazil	1953–1986; 1993–on
New Zealand	1954–1972
Belgium	1954–1975
Australia	1954–1976
Mexico	1955–on
Philippines	1959–1982
Uruguay	1961–1987
Venezuela	1963–1981
Portugal	1964–1976
Costa Rica	1966–1975
Peru	1966–1987
Singapore	1968–1974
Malaysia	1968–1977
Thailand	1972–1974
Indonesia	1972–1976
Yugoslavia	1973–1976
Nigeria	1975–1987

as they were sold to foreign visitors only. In 1952, he obtained a licence to import Volkswagens, which he offered to visiting American servicemen stationed on the US airbases and, over the following year, he sold about twenty cars. It looked likely that the regulations would be relaxed to allow cars to be imported for sale to the general public, and Colborne-Baber visited Wolfsburg to negotiate taking on the Volkswagen concession in the UK. But events took an unusual turn, as he later recalled:

> I virtually had permission from the Board of Trade that I would be allowed to import cars for sale to the general public, and discussing this in the factory on a Saturday morning the export manager said, 'Can you get in touch with your Board of Trade and let us speak to them and have this confirmed?' Of course it was Saturday morning and the Board of Trade weren't at work, so this was quashed for the moment. They said 'We will send out a representative to come and visit you and discuss the matter on your home ground'.
>
> I told the representative to come and stay in London and made reservations for him, but he didn't turn up. The following morning he called us to say that he was staying with Steve O'Flaherty in London (O'Flaherty was the director of Irish Motor Distributors, who held the Volkswagen concession in Eire). Steve had happened to fly over on the same plane as him.

The next day Colborne-Baber went to the Berkeley Hotel in London to meet the elusive factory representative. Unfortunately, recalled Colborne-Baber, this rep turned out to be:

> so drunk he didn't know what he was talking about. He was almost carried out of

to buy any German products at all.

As we've seen, the first UK Beetles were personal imports, a number of which were refurbished and sold by motor dealer John Colborne-Baber. Importing new cars to sell in the UK was at that time not permitted, but Colborne-Baber made use of a loophole which allowed cars to be imported as long

Beetles imported to the UK arrived at Ramsgate docks ready assembled and covered in a thick coating of protective wax. Then came the delicate operation of lifting them onto dry land by crane.

the Berkeley by the commissionaire. I took him to the train at Euston, he staggered into the carriage and sat down and said 'Well Mr Baber, you want a contract rather like Mr O'Flaherty's got in Dublin and you'll be hearing from the factory very shortly, rest assured'. The next thing was

that I got a letter saying that O'Flaherty had got the lot.

Despite this disappointment, Colborne-Baber didn't lose his enthusiasm for the Beetle, and the car dealership he started retains close links with VW to this day. But for the time being responsibility for the task of selling the Beetle in the UK passed to O'Flaherty. He set up VW Motors Ltd at Bedford Street in London, and placed an initial order for 200 right-hand-drive cars, each accompanied by £10-worth of spares.

Sales were sluggish to begin with, and in the whole of 1953 VW Motors shifted only 945 units. But soon people began to appreciate what great value for money the Beetle provided, and antipathy towards its German origins started to fade. The following year sales went up to 3,260, and by the start of the 1960s they averaged 16,000 per year, ensuring the Beetle's place in the affections of the British public.

BEETLE MEETS AMERICA

Across the Atlantic the story followed similar lines. Given time, America grew to love the Beetle, elevating it to a cult status it achieved nowhere else in the world. But the early days were sticky ones for Volkswagen, and although Nordhoff clearly recognized the potential of such a vast market, he must sometimes have despaired at the challenge of getting the Americans to accept a vehicle which was so unlike anything they were used to driving.

The first attempt to break into the American market was made not directly by Volkswagen, but by Dutch importer Ben Pon. As early as January 1949, Pon had taken a standard grey saloon to New York, sailing across the Atlantic from Rotterdam. Pon toured dealerships with his Beetle, but encountered a depressing lack of interest.

Americans were poised to embark on a consumerist boom, a time when bigger meant better and materialism ruled. The American automobile of the 1950s was to be a gargantuan, dazzling, over-styled, gas-guzzling lounge-on-wheels. Not surprising-

ly, American dealers looked in disdain at the modestly styled, basic and thrifty Beetle, and saw no place for such a car in their American dream. Bitterly disappointed, Pon sold his sample Beetle for $950 and returned home.

Nordhoff, however, was not to be dissuaded so easily. In Easter 1949 he travelled to America, taking with him not a Beetle but promotional pictures and drawings of the car. The customs officers who examined these at New York airport were amazed. 'No one in the world would buy a car that looked like that!' they cried out.

The potential dealers whom Nordhoff visited reacted in much the same way, and like Ben Pon before him, he received a poor response to his efforts to promote the car. However, he did make the breakthrough of establishing an official import agency with New York dealer Max Hoffman. The Beetle made an odd contrast for Hoffman, who specialized in importing prestige European marques – a description that could hardly be applied to VW at the time.

Volkswagens started to trickle onto American roads: 157 in 1950, 390 in 1951, 601 in 1952 and 980 in 1953. It was hardly an impressive sales performance. Like most Americans who had seen the Beetle, Hoffman seemed to have concluded that this tiny, unconventional foreign car would never gain any sort of mass appeal in the US, and was reluctant to waste time promoting it.

Nordhoff disagreed. At the end of 1953 he cancelled Hoffman's franchise and set up Volkswagen-owned bases on both coasts of America, in New York and San Francisco. Nordhoff dressed two young salesmen in jeans, and told them to tour the small towns of America singling out the more youthful, go-ahead, motor dealers.

The strategy was an immediate success. Volkswagen gained new dealers across the country. Sales leapt to 6,343 in 1954, and then soared to 35,851 the following year, making the US Volkswagen's most important export market. Of the 51,000 cars imported to the US in 1955, 34,000 were Volkswagens. Demand started outstripping supply, and waiting lists several months long became commonplace. Beetles were imported unofficially to make up the shortfall, and between 1958 and 1960 these 'bootleg Beetles' constituted up to twenty per cent of overall sales.

The Beetle carved out its own distinct niche in American society. It appealed on a number of levels. Young people looking for a cheap, economical car loved it, whilst the more well-off saw it as an ideal second car and liberals adopted it as a welcome alternative to those wasteful, swaggering Buicks, Chevys and Pontiacs.

American car manufacturers prided themselves on making each year's model bigger, brasher and flashier than the year before's. Because fashions changed so rapidly it was obvious to everyone when you were driving last year's model – and wasn't it about time you traded up? Under the hoods of these behemoths were enormous V8 engines that guzzled gas like tomorrow didn't exist. Not everyone shared these values, and the Beetle had a strong appeal to those who wanted to keep their lives simpler and less wasteful.

In time even Hollywood took to the Beetle as the ultimate in inverted snobbery. The Beetle became a trendy car to be seen in, and from there it was a short step to mass-market success. US motoring magazine *Road & Track* said in 1956:

The Beetle has done what no other vehicle manufactured outside the USA has ever been able to do; it has gained an unmistakable wheelhold in the garages and hearts of the American car-buying public.

The VW fulfils a need which Detroit had forgotten existed – a need for a car that is cheap to buy and run, small and compact, light and manoeuvrable, yet solidly constructed, and, perhaps above all, utterly dependable and trouble-free.

US manufacturers fought back in the 1960s by launching their own compact cars. These hit European models hard. From 614,000 in 1960, imported car sales fell to 339,000 two years later. But by now the Beetle was too well established to be affected. Other European models such as the Morris Minor were practically wiped out of the US market – but the Beetle went on from strength to strength.

One big factor in the Beetle's success was the skilful, innovative and uniquely appropriate advertising campaign that was run in the US to promote it. This campaign was orchestrated by Doyle Dane Bernbach (DDB), a small, creative and unconventional agency appointed by VW in 1959.

DDB's advertising succeeded precisely because it was so different from other American car advertising. Which made sense, since the Beetle was so different from other American cars. Their ads took a down-to-earth tone that emphasized the practical qualities of the Beetle.

There were no scenes of cars posed in front of posh hotels, with suave drivers and their sexy girlfriends, of the type that were normally used in an effort to boost a model's status and glamour. Instead, the Beetle ads deliberately understated the appeal of their car, and threw in a touch of self-deprecating humour for good measure. 'It's ugly, but it gets you there' declared one ad. 'Live below your means', and 'Think small', said others. 'After a few years it starts to look beautiful' said yet another, stressing the Beetle's long-term durability. Readers felt they were being talked to intelligently, instead of being fed the usual hard-sell spiel.

VW's executive in the US, Carl Hahn, later explained:

> Our advertising campaign would have been wrong to express anything but unpretentiousness and modesty, given the fact that the VW looks unpretentious and modest from the outside. Precisely because we are able to talk about our product in a language that is easily understood, we are able to address customers who have had enough of everlasting superlatives and hyperbolic fantasy.

The ads won DDB a string of creative awards, and more importantly they got results. They set the Beetle on a roll that saw sales in the US grow more than sevenfold in the decade from 1958. In 1968, VW of America had its best year ever, selling 390,379 Beetle saloons and 9,595 Cabriolets. 'Why do so many people buy Volkswagens?' asked VW publicity, in typical tongue-in-cheek mode. 'In our first year we sold two cars – since then we've sold 2,000,000.'

VOLKSWAGEN'S SALES PHILOSOPHY

Back home in Germany, once Nordhoff began to realize the massive sales potential open to the Beetle, he set out in clear terms the direction which Volkswagen would take. Up till now a number of companies had collaborated with Volkswagen to build a variety of vehicles based on the Beetle. Miesen, for instance, made Beetle-derived ambulances, and Hebmüller produced spartan open police cars. An even greater range of Beetle-based vehicles had been turned out by coachbuilders working independently of Volkswagen.

Nordhoff decided that from now on Volkswagen would concentrate on promot-

Hebmüller's Beetle-based police car must have been a draughty means of transport in winter.

Type 2 – the ever-practical Transporter

The Type 2, or VW Transporter, became a success story in its own way as impressive as the Beetle's. Like the latter, the Transporter was a practical, no-frills vehicle that carved out its own niche in the marketplace, filled that niche perfectly and in spite of its imitators, established a cult following among its fans that endures to this day.

The Transporter's origins stem from early attempts to develop a commercial derivative of the Beetle. In Germany in the late 1940s, there was a great demand for such vehicles, but due to its rear-engined layout, the Beetle chassis wasn't the easiest to convert into a van, as the engine obstructed rear access.

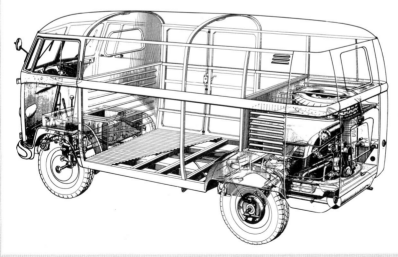

Outside and inside a Type 2 Transporter. The Type 2's ingenious division of weight, with the driver at the front and engine at the back, meant heavy loads could be carried in the central bay without upsetting the vehicle's balance.

Several types of Beetle-based van had been made, but none was a great success. Volkswagen took the decision to approach the idea of a commercial Beetle derivative in earnest, and came up with a design of beguiling simplicity. The body was fashioned as a simple box, with the driver sitting up above the front axle, the engine tucked away at the rear and the centre reserved for a surprisingly capacious load space accessed through side doors.

Early prototypes used the Beetle chassis, but when this was found to lack the necessary torsional strength a purpose-designed chassis was substituted, with a pair of hefty box sections running lengthways along it. The Beetle's familiar running gear and torsion bar suspension were retained.

With the payload concentrated in the centre of the vehicle, the Transporter was stable even when heavily laden. It proved itself as a practical and effective load-carrier, able to transport almost its own weight in cargo. As the original 25bhp engine struggled to propel these sorts of loads, reduction gearing (as used on the Kübelwagen) was fitted to the rear hubs to help it up the hills. Fully laden, it could manage 50mph (80km/h).

At its launch in 1950 the Type 2 was offered as a closed van (the Kombi) or eight-seater minibus, with a variety of body styles being added to the range over the following years. In 1956 VW set up a factory in Hanover solely for Transporter production, and by the end of the 1970s more than five million had been made. Ultimately the torsion bar suspension was superseded by a coil-spring setup, and water-cooling was introduced for the engine.

In its air-cooled days the Type 2 remained closely linked to the Beetle, and it was often used as a test-bed for Beetle development. The 34bhp version of the 1,200 engine and the twelve-volt electrical system both saw a year's service in the Type 2 before they were adopted by the Beetle.

ing the Beetle saloon, and not divert its resources into developing new projects. This wasn't a rule cast in stone – VW's own Beetle-derived van, the Type 2 Transporter, became an increasingly important sideshoot to production, and collaboration with Karmann brought about the Karmann Ghia coupé. But these were deviations from Nordhoff's overriding objective, which was to perfect and sell the Beetle.

At the same time Nordhoff cracked down on the practice of supplying independent coachbuilders with Beetle running chassis on which to base their specials, stating unequivocally in 1954: 'This is a car factory, not a chassis factory. We wish to retain control over the appearance of cars that carry the company name. Simply supplying chassis alone is of no interest to us whatsoever.'

The supply of chassis dried up, which meant that coachbuilders had to buy new Beetles whole, dismantle them and sell off the redundant bodies as spares. Many found this unprofitable, but even so a remarkable variety of rebodied Beetles were born during the 1950s, until the advent of cheap and adaptable glassfibre gave the business of customizing Beetle running gear a whole new kick of life in the following decade.

Hand in hand with Nordhoff's strategy of concentrating on the existing Beetle, rather than developing new models, came a dedication to evolution that would have made Charles Darwin envious. Volkswagen embarked on an on-going programme of detailed design improvements for the Beetle – each new model year brought with it dozens of small, but often significant, improvements.

Many of these changes took place under the skin, so to the uninitiated the Beetle appeared to change hardly at all. When the final German-built Beetle rolled off its production line in 1978, no one would have hesitated in identifying it as essentially the

Type 2 Transporter

Engine
Type	Air-cooled flat-four
Capacity	1,192cc
Bore × stroke	77mm × 64mm
Compression ratio	6.6:1
Max. power	30bhp @ 3,400rpm
Max. torque	56lb/ft @ 2,000rpm

Transmission
Gearbox	Manual four-speed, synchro on second, third, fourth, reduction gearing

Suspension
Front	Independent with transverse torsion bars and trailing arms
Rear	Independent with swing axles, transverse torsion bars

Brakes
	Drum all-round

Dimensions (in/mm)
Length	165/4,191
Width	76/1,941
Weight	2,315lb (1,050kg)

Performance
Top speed	59mph (94km/h)
Fuel consumption	30mpg (9.4l/100km)

Efficient mass-production techniques were an important factor in the Beetle's success, helping to keep costs down. This factory scene from the 1950s shows body presses stamping out wings to be transfered automatically down the line.

*Body assembly on a line of
Beetles that stretches away into
the distance.*

*Prime coating of Beetle bodies in
a dip tank at Wolfsburg.*

Mounting of bodies on their chassis on the final assembly line.

same car as the Beetle which Nordhoff took on when he joined Volkswagen in 1949. Yet such was the scale of the modifications that had taken place that the two cars shared only one minor component – the clamping strip that retained the bonnet and engine lid rubber seals.

During Nordhoff's early years the policy of evolution had been a necessary continuation of the development work the British had carried out after the war simply to turn the Beetle into a serviceable vehicle. The car Nordhoff had inherited was by no means perfect. It had, as Nordhoff memorably described it, 'more faults than a dog has fleas'. But he recognized the basic soundness of Porsche's design. His task was to polish this flawed diamond until it

sparkled.

This strategy ran counter to accepted practice among major motor manufacturers, who as they launched one model would already be designing a successor to replace it once it had been declared obsolete four or five years down the line. As a car that flew in the face of this profligate trend, the Beetle was green before its time.

Nordhoff's other great achievement came in streamlining production methods, turning the Wolfsburg factory into a model of efficient mass-production.

When he took over in 1948, each car took 400 hours to build. 'If we go on like this,' declared Nordhoff, 'we won't be going on much longer. We must get it down to 100 hours per vehicle.' Workers looked astound-

Fifty Years of Beetle Production

Year	Annual Beetle production (all models)	Annual Beetle Cabriolet production
1945	1,785	
1946	10,020	
1947	8,987	
1948	19,244	3
1949	46,146	364
1950	81,979	2,695
1951	93,709	3,938
1952	114,348	4,763
1953	151,323	4,256
1954	202,174	4,740
1955	279,986	6,361
1956	333,190	6,868
1957	380,561	8,196
1958	451,526	9,624
1959	575,406	10,995
1960	739,443	11,921
1961	827,850	12,005
1962	877,014	10,129
1963	838,488	10,599
1964	948,370	10,355
1965	1,090,863	10,754
1966	1,080,165	9,712
1967	925,787	7,583
1968	1,186,134	13,386
1969	1,219,314	15,802
1970	1,196,099	18,008
1971	1,291,612	24,317
1972	1,220,686	14,865
1973	1,206,018	17,685
1974	791,053	12,694
1975	441,116	5,327
1976	383,277	11,081
1977	258,634	14,218
1978	271,673	18,511
1979	263,340	19,569
1980	236,177	544
1981	157,505	
1982	138,091	
1983	119,745	
1984	118,138	
1985	86,189	
1986	46,633	
1987	17,166	
1988	19,008	
1989	32,421	
1990	84,716	

1991	85,681	
1992	86,158	
1993	99,931	
1994	98,209	
1995	42,000	
Total	21,275,100	331,868

ed on hearing this unlikely sounding goal, but by 1955 it had been achieved. Improvements in efficiency actually allowed a price cut for the Beetle that year.

The Volkswagen factory became a key player in Germany's post-war economic miracle, the *Wirtschaftwunder.* As *Time* magazine commented, 'Nowhere is the recovery of the Germans more obvious than in Germany's number one car factory, the Volkswagenwerk, and its boss, Herr Nordhoff.' In 1955, the year of the millionth Beetle, Wolfsburg took on 6,000 extra employees, had 970 German dealerships and 2,498 abroad, and accounted for almost half of all German car exports. In 1956 a new factory was opened at Hanover, to build the Transporter which was itself now creating a substantial demand. More new factories followed at Kassel and Emden. The production lines were moving flat-out to meet demand.

Even though the Beetle was on its way to becoming the economic marvel of the decade, some voices were already beginning to question Nordhoff's one-model strategy. Dealers wanted to know when extra models would arrive to flesh out the Volkswagen range and capitalize on the Beetle's success.

Nordhoff had little time for such distractions. When asked by *Der Spiegel* why Volkswagen had no new model to show for 1959, but only the twenty-five-year-old Beetle, he replied waspishly, 'It should not be the aim of the motor industry simply to

bring out new models, but rather to build cars and sell them. We are just starting on the fourth million in the production life of the Volkswagen you criticize so sharply'.

Not that Nordhoff considered the idea of a successor to the Beetle totally unthinkable. Wolfsburg's development department produced a series of prototypes designed either to replace the Beetle, or to sit alongside it as a larger or smaller model. With the all-conquering Beetle in the background, it was no surprise that most tended to be based around a rear-engined, air-cooled design – and that with the Beetle continuing to sell so well, few of these prototypes came in for serious consideration.

Nordhoff's innate conservatism, becoming more pronounced as he grew older, was a powerful force against change. A larger car, he argued, wouldn't represent such good value as a Beetle. And as for demands for a smaller, cheaper car – well, people could just buy a secondhand Beetle, he retorted.

VW TYPE 3

Ultimately, however, Nordhoff bowed to the inevitable and introduced a newcomer to the Volkswagen range, the Type 3, at the 1961 Frankfurt Show. It was roomier and more conventionally styled than the Beetle, but it was powered – naturally – by an air-cooled rear-mounted boxer engine. The Type 3 wasn't an obvious successor to the Beetle, and it sold alongside it as a slightly more upmarket, medium-sized, model. If anyone had hoped that the Type 3 would one day replace the Beetle, it certainly wouldn't happen in a hurry. By 1961 the Beetle was selling over 800,000 units worldwide and production was growing every year.

On paper, the Type 3 was in many ways a superior vehicle to the Beetle. But for all

Beetle production accelerated at an unstoppable rate in the sixties. The five million mark was passed in 1962, and the ten millionth Beetle rolled off the production line just five years later.

Type 3 – the Beetle replacement that never was

Designed to meet a growing demand for roomier family cars, the Type 3 took the basic Beetle formula of rear-engined flat-four engine and torsion bar suspension, and added a list of ingredients that made it an apparently superior, more practical vehicle than the Beetle.

For a start, the Type 3 Notchback saloon, which was launched at the Frankfurt motor show in 1961, had bodywork styled much more in keeping with the fashion of the time than that of the ageing Beetle. Its engine, the familiar flat-four, had been increased in capacity to 1,493cc, which gave the Notchback a decent turn of speed.

Modifications made to the Type 3's flat-four engine meant it really earned its name – by fitting a redesigned fan, carburettor and other ancillaries, the overall height of the engine was reduced to just 38cm. It was fitted low down at the rear of the chassis, where it was accessible through a trapdoor. With this closed, there was a handy extra luggage space in addition to the rear boot.

Roadholding and handling were superior to the Beetle's, with better resistance to crosswinds, visibility was considerably improved, and the Type 3 was a lot more refined and comfortable. Its appeal was increased by the addition of a twin-carb 1500S and a practical Variant estate in 1963, and again in 1965 when the 1600TL Fastback was introduced.

Type 3 Fastbacks, Notchbacks and Variants were decent cars by the standards of their day, and sold in their millions, but they didn't have the Beetle's ability to appeal to all levels of class, age and society.

That year, 1965, also saw the first Type 3 sold in the US – where VW had thus far held back in order not to harm Beetle sales. In 1967 fuel-injection and a three-speed auto were also offered. US magazine *Motor Trend* compared the new VW1600 to the Beetle and found it 'just a little bit more of everything – faster, bigger, quieter, and more deluxe throughout'.

But for all its abilities, the Type 3 never sold as briskly as VW had hoped. Its higher cost moved it into a price-bracket where it competed with a wide range of middle-market cars. In October 1966, a 1600TL Fastback cost £1,016, a 1600L Variant £1,077. Either of these represented a much greater investment than a 1500 Beetle, which cost just £697. As one American magazine put it, 'Going, stopping, handling and riding are all better – but are these qualities enough to justify a $700 higher price?'

Although the Type 3 retained a lot of the drawbacks of the Beetle's design, it possessed little of the Beetle's charm, and it lacked the Beetle's unique ability to combine simple ingredients into a whole that was so much more special than its constituent parts.

From today's viewpoint the Type 3 is sometimes looked back on as a failure, a rather unfair accusation considering that by the time production ended in 1973 more than 2.5 million had been built – a total that easily beats some established classics such as the Morris Minor. It just seemed to be a sales flop, in the light of the inevitable comparison with the Beetle which consistently over-shadowed and outsold its younger brother.

Type 3

Engine

Type	Air-cooled flat-four
Capacity	1,493cc
Bore × stroke	83mm × 69mm
Compression ratio	7.2:1
Max. power	53bhp @ 4,000rpm
Max. torque	83lb/ft @ 2,000rpm

Transmission

Gearbox	Manual four-speed, synchro on all forward gears

Suspension

Front	Independent with transverse torsion bars and trailing arms
Rear	Independent with swing axles, transverse torsion bars

Brakes

Drum all-round

Dimensions (in/mm)

Length	166/4,220
Width	63/1,600
Weight	1,960lb (890kg)

Performance

0–60mph	21sec
Top speed	82mph (131km/h)
Fuel consumption	27mpg (10.5l/100km)

There were echoes of the wartime Kübelwagen in the Type 181. Designed for general-purpose military use, it also became popular in California, where enthusiasts nicknamed it the 'Thing'.

its abilities the Type 3 lacked the Beetle's charm, and it failed to capture the public's affections like the Beetle had done. Its sales performance never came close to beating the Beetle, which outsold the Type 3 by about five to one throughout its twelve-year production life.

Although the Type 3 didn't supply the answer to the question of the Beetle's successor, Nordhoff didn't see any reason to panic yet. Beetle production in Germany hit a blip in 1963, when home sales dropped for the first time, and production fell by 40,000 to 838,000. But by the following year the Beetle was back on course, and in 1965 annual production exceeded one million for the first time.

The occasional minor variation on the Beetle theme continued to see the light of day. There was the Fridolin, a van designed for the West German post office, but which

on the second-hand market became popular as a cut-price camper, and the Type 181, an austere general-purpose vehicle reminiscent of the Kübelwagen. This was designed for Army use, but soon became popular among younger drivers, especially in America where it was fondly nicknamed the 'Thing'.

VW TYPE 4

In the late 1960s work began on the design of a larger, more upmarket, Volkswagen model, the Type 4. This was an ill-conceived foray into territory which would have been better left to Audi (which VW had taken over in 1965) and it did nothing to lessen VW's dependence on the Beetle.

It was the events of 1967 that brought the sharpest attacks yet on Nordhoff's poli-

Type 4 – a Volkswagen with class

The Type 4 represented an attempt by Volkswagen to establish a foothold in more upmarket territory. But because it drew heavily on the legacy of the Beetle, the Type 4 retained too many of that car's quirky features to compete successfully against the more conventional designs that dominated the executive market.

Although it was launched in 1968, the Type 4, or VW411 as it was ultimately called, still used an air-cooled flat-four engine derived from the Beetle's venerable unit. In 411 guise, capacity was increased to 1,679cc and it turned out 68bhp. But because the 411 was, at 2,249lb (1,020kg), a considerably heavier car than the Beetle, its performance was decidedly mediocre for its class. Top speed was under 90mph (145km/h), and 0–60mph came up in around 16 seconds. Yet its fuel consumption wasn't particularly impressive either.

In other ways the 411 represented a real advance for VW. It was the company's first model to dispense with a separate chassis, and the first mainstream VW model to have four doors. Luggage capacity – which like the Type 3's, was split between front and rear compartments – was generous. The spacious Variant Estate version proved particularly popular.

MacPherson struts were used in the front suspension, several years before they found their way onto the Super Beetle, while the rear suspension employed double-jointed axles to give safe, reliable, handling.

Inside, the 411 was refined and comfortable. It even boasted a petrol-burning heater that could be programmed up to twenty-four hours in advance. This could be warming up the car while you were still munching your cornflakes – an ability many Beetle owners must have envied.

One of the least happy aspects of the 411 was its styling, particularly the broad, bland nose with two elongated headlamps. This was soon modified by VW, who substituted a neater twin-headlamp front end. Fuel injection was also fitted, a rare feature for the time. This hiked the power output to 80bhp, but inadequate performance remained a strong criticism of the 411. VW's quality

VW's attempt to move upmarket, the 411, had some interesting features but lacked the refinement and prestige to compete against the likes of Mercedes and BMW.

control also seemed to have slipped on this model, which started to gain an unfortunate reputation for unreliability and premature rusting.

A facelifted Type 4 appeared in late 1972, badged the 412. Its redesigned, sleeker front end helped improve aerodynamics and reduce fuel consumption, but by this time the end was in sight for the Type 4. It was discontinued in 1974, having sold just 350,000. The model had achieved little but to dabble in territory VW would henceforth leave its Audi marque to develop, and to divert resources away from the real dilemma that faced VW – how to replace the Beetle?

Type 4

Engine

Type	Air-cooled flat-four
Capacity	1,679cc
Bore × stroke	90mm × 66mm
Compression ratio	7.8:1
Max. power	68bhp @ 4,500rpm
Max. torque	92lb/ft @ 2,000rpm

Transmision

Gearbox	Manual four-speed, synchro on all forward gears

Suspension

Front	Independent with coil springs
Rear	Independent with coil springs

Brakes

Front disc, rear drum

Dimensions (in/mm)

Length	180/4,560
Width	65/1,640
Weight	2,250lb (1,020kg)

Performance

0–60mph	16sec
Top speed	87mph (139km/h)
Fuel consumption	23mpg (12.3l/100km)

cies. A combination of rising taxes, fuel prices and insurance premiums caused a slump in home demand, while the Deutschmark hardened against the dollar, and this hit sales in America. Nordhoff was forced to put the Wolfsburg workforce, accustomed for as long as anyone could remember to working at full capacity, on short working for forty-two days. German production that year fell below 819,000, and Fiat edged out VW as the top European car manufacturer

Dealers, shareholders, bankers, politicians and journalists all raised their voices against Nordhoff. 'VW has been asleep', accused one paper. German finance minister Franz-Josef Strauss criticized Nordhoff, challenging him to build better cars.

Nordhoff was defensive. 'You see for yourself what vitality there is hidden in this car, which has been pronounced dead more often than all those designs of which hardly a memory remains.' But sadly for Nordhoff, his own vitality was running out. His hard-working lifestyle was taking its toll. He suffered from stomach ulcers and after a series of heart attacks he died in 1968, at the age of sixty-nine.

Nordhoff's achievements had been immense. Over ten million Beetles had been produced during his reign. Despite the criticisms, his belief in the Beetle was further vindicated as sales figures rallied again as the decade changed, reaching an all-time high of 1,219,000 in 1971. With hindsight, it was Volkswagen's concern with launching new models in the mid-1960s that had contributed to the Beetle's development being neglected and sales slipping as a consequence.

In 1972, Beetle production beat the record of 15,007,033 units set by Ford's Model T in 1927.

Volkswagen now appreciated that the Beetle had to be kept competitive with the newer models that were continually appearing. They started to address the situation by introducing a series of major improvements. To give the Beetle more competitive performance, a 1300 engine was introduced in 1965, and a 1500 arrived the following year. The Beetle underwent a facelift, gaining important updates such as twelve-volt electrics and the option of a semi-automatic gearbox.

In 1970 the Super Beetle was launched, with more powerful twin-port engines and a new MacPherson strut front suspension, which offered a significant gain in luggage space under the front bonnet. The Super Beetles proved to be immensely popular, and with their help production reached record levels in the early 1970s.

SUCCESSORS TO THE BEETLE

Nevertheless, Volkswagen now had real cause to be worried. The Type 3 and Type 4 were both reaching the end of their production lives. And while the Beetle in 1972 was still selling well, it was running flat-out to keep up with the rapid advances in car design and increasingly stringent safety and emissions legislation. If the experience of Ford's Model T, the century's other mass-selling car, was anything to go by, when the public did eventually tire of the Beetle its sales would be in danger of slumping catastrophically.

The main direction in which Volkswagen had been developing was in acquiring other companies. Auto-Union came under the VW umbrella in 1965, and the Audi marque was reactivated, giving VW an entrance into the middle-market sector. In 1969 VW bought a major shareholding in NSU, whose quirky rotary-engined designs quickly proved more of a liability than a benefit.

The situation was becoming critical for VW. New model development was vital to take the marque into the 1970s. Work had been commissioned on the development of a Beetle successor from Porsche, who had maintained their close links with Volkswagen over the years.

Like VW, Porsche had a strong tradition of rear-engined models, and its proposals for the Beetle replacement reflected this. Its engineers rejected the front-engined layout as having 'too many technical weaknesses', and came up instead with the EA266. Prototypes featured an engine mounted over the rear axle, squeezed in beneath the rear seats. Access to the engine was severely restricted – the dipstick had to be more than a metre in length – typical rear-engined handling problems were encountered and noise levels proved to be uncomfortably high.

Most importantly, the EA266 represented a serious misreading of motoring trends. The 1970s was the decade when front-wheel drive gained wide acceptance as the most suitable layout for volume produced cars, both on grounds of safety and packaging. If it had been allowed to go into production, it's hard to imagine that the EA266 would have been anything other than a flop, with possibly disastrous effects on Volkswagen as a company.

For a time, it looked as though the EA266 would go ahead. Despite its problems, so much money had been poured into the project that the thought of cancelling it was hard to contemplate. However, this is precisely what new Board Chairman Rudolf Leiding did, bravely stepping in to stop work on the model just as it was about to go into production.

Fortunately, Leiding had an ace to play. Volkswagen's own engineers had been

Porsche's suggested Beetle-replacement, the EA266. With a rear-engined design that was at odds with the trend towards front-engined cars, the EA266 threatened to be a sales flop. Production was cancelled in the nick of time, in favour of a front-engined alternative, the EA276 Golf prototype.

working on their own ideas for a Beetle successor, the EA276. This had spacious hatchback packaging, a front water-cooled engine, and bodywork neatly styled by Italian designer Giugiaro. It was launched as the Golf in 1974, and since then has deservedly gone on to achieve immense popularity and sales success.

Interestingly, at one stage VW's engineers were considering fitting the Beetle's air-cooled flat-four in the Golf – such a model, badged the Gol, did in fact go on sale in Brazil in 1980.

Alongside the Golf came other models, the Polo and Passat, which followed the same front-engined, water-cooled path. They arrived in the nick of time. In 1974, for the first time in its history, VW made a loss, of some £142.5 million, and the shock

waves went deep. But a combination of cool-headedness, clear-thinking and engineering excellence had saved the day. From its perilous situation at the turn of the decade, when over-dependence on the Beetle saw Volkswagen poised on the brink of disaster, the company regained a position of real strength from which to face the 1980s and beyond.

THE BEETLE TAKES A BACK SEAT

With both Volkswagen's and the public's attention increasingly focused on these new water-cooled models, Beetle sales began to fall off rapidly. German production fell from 895,000 in 1973 to 451,000

Unofficial Volkswagens

By the time Beetle production started again after World War Two, the writing was on the wall for the traditional coachbuilder. In the early days of the motor car, it had been common practice for prospective owners to buy a bare running chassis, and then commission a coachbuilder to clothe it in bodywork. More affluent owners could afford to commission one-off bodies tailored to their own requirements, but coachbuilders also offered designs that could be bought off the peg.

What ultimately killed the traditional coachbuilder, hand-crafting in steel or aluminium, was the advent of glassfibre which could be quickly and easily moulded to form cheap, lightweight bodies. Glassfibre didn't become widely used till the 1960s, but even in the early 1950s coachbuilders were starting to find their traditional supply routes drying up. By then it was the norm for car companies to sell their models fully bodied. It became increasingly difficult to get hold of chassis, as manufacturers turned to monocoque designs in which the body contributed an integral part of the car's overall rigidity.

The Beetle falls between modern monocoque and traditional independent chassis designs. Its body provides some degree of rigidity to an otherwise lightweight, flexible chassis. But nonetheless, it quickly established itself as a favourite choice for coachbuilders. As long as the bodywork was well braced, flexing wasn't too much of a problem. The only difficulty was a political one – Nordhoff's unwillingness to provide rolling chassis to any but a small and carefully vetted selection of coachbuilders.

'Coachbuilders' is a loose term. Special-bodied Beetles ranged from one-offs built by skilled amateurs (many of which have long since rusted into obscurity) to series-built models from established companies, such as Rometsch, who built a Beetle-based roadster.

Rometsch exemplified the high quality that could be expected from the best coachbuilders. Its roadster – a two-seater known affectionately as the Banana because of its curved profile – won a Golden Rose of Geneva three years running in recognition of the quality of its bodywork. Constructed in aluminium, each roadster took about 1,000 hours to complete. Sadly, the Berlin-based company had to close after the Berlin Wall, erected with shocking speed in August 1961, isolated the factory in the west of the city from most of its skilled workforce who lived in the east.

Rometsch's stylish and meticulously hand-crafted 'Banana' roadster was one of the many coachbuilt models based on Beetle running gear in the 1950s, despite problems of chassis supply from an unco-operative VW.

Among the other major coachbuilt Beetle variations of the 1950s were:

Beutler
Swiss company Beutler built a number of variations on the Beetle theme. Best known is the sports car, available as a coupé or a convertible, that was launched at the 1954 Geneva Motor Show. Practical, elegant and superbly executed, the car had a distinctive Mercedes-style front grille. Beutler offered their own twin-carb conversion, but some cars were fitted with the engine from the Porsche 356.

Dannenhauer and Stauss
This Stuttgart company built open-top roadsters with simple lines that echoed the Porsche 356. Unusually, they were constructed from steel and had rear-hinged 'suicide' doors. Around 100 cars were produced between 1951 and 1956. Taking 800-1,000 hours to build, they were expensive compared with the Karmann Ghia.

Denzel
Austrian engineer Wolfgang Denzel first produced a lightweight wooden-bodied Beetle sports car in the late 1940s – and won the 1949 Austrian Alpine Rally in it! With further racing in mind, he built a series of 350 sports cars – in aluminium this time – with the option of a tuned 1,290cc 64bhp competition engine. The last car was made in 1959.

Drews
The three Drews brothers produced one of the earliest Beetle-based specials. This open roadster was an ornate if rather squarely styled vehicle, with aluminium bodywork and external trim, and an awkward split front windscreen. It featured a flat-topped steering wheel to aid visibility. A high price for this hand-crafted car kept production numbers down, and by the end of the run in 1951 only 150 had been made.

Enzmann
Enzmann produced a roadster ahead of its time, a car that was designed in 1953 but whose sleek styling today looks more like a product of the 1960s. It also broke new ground as one of the first Beetle-based specials to feature a glassfibre body. One drawback was that the car lacked doors, which would have weakened the body structure. With styling that refused to date, the Enzmann remained successfully on sale till 1968.

Wendler
Soon after the war this long-established coachbuilder produced an appealing Beetle-based 'Woody' station wagon. Better known, however, were its sports cars, again Beetle-based and strongly reminiscent of the Porsche 356. Doors, however, were rear-hinged in suicide style. Cars were produced on an individual commission basis and few were made.

the following year, and down to 114,000 in 1975. Faced with increasingly strict emissions regulations, the Super Beetle was dropped in the US in 1976, though the 1200 was sold there for another year, badged as the 'classic' Beetle.

VW began to regard the Beetle as taking up valuable production line space that could be used more profitably. Its traditional home, Wolfsburg, built its last Beetle in

End of an era – the last German-made Beetle leaves the Emden production line in January 1978.

July 1974, and German production shifted to the VW plant at Emden.

The Beetle still had its loyal fans, who continued to buy Beetles despite the arrival of the new generation of Volkswagen models, and the repeated pruning of the Beetle range. But demand was shrinking fast – Beetle registrations in Britain totalled just 389 in 1978.

With Beetle production still going strong in Mexico, VW realized they could satisfy the remaining European demand by importing Mexican-built Beetles. The last European-built Beetle saloon left Emden on 19 January 1978, closing a forty-year chapter of German Beetle production. In its place came the first imports of Mexican saloons, fitted with the 1200 engine.

This wasn't the absolute end of Beetle production in Europe. Continuing demand for the Beetle Cabriolet, particularly from the US, saw production of this model continue for another two years at Karmann's Osnabrück factory. Finally, that too came to a close on 10 January 1980, by which time some 330,000 Cabriolets had been built.

It had been a glorious history, and one that had surpassed even the high expectations of its designer Ferdinand Porsche. More remarkably still, the Beetle story by no means ended with the finish of European production. This seemingly immortal car lived on in Mexico and Brazil, where production continues to this day.

6 Early Days: Splits and Ovals

When the world's press were given their chance to drive the Beetle for the very first time in February 1939, Britain's motoring pundits arrived not knowing quite what to make of this strange-looking car which was being produced under highly suspicious circumstances. Was the whole thing nothing more than a Nazi publicity stunt?

A short drive was all it took to convince them otherwise. *Motor's* correspondent heaped praise on the Beetle's phenomenal cornering abilities, comfortable suspension and powerful brakes. So capable was the car, in fact, that some pundits began to express concern about the possibility of the Beetle, competitively priced thanks to its massive state backing, knocking a serious dent in Britain's own motor industry.

Not that they thought the Beetle was perfect. Its top gear acceleration was considered lethargic, it was felt to be unduly noisy, and its basic interior was slated as crude by UK standards. And one thing commentators seemed unanimous on was the car's styling. Astonishing as it might seem to today's Beetle enthusiast, in the thirties and forties most people considered the Beetle to be downright ugly. If it sold at all, they said, it would be despite, not because of, its styling.

As the passing years proved, the Beetle was simply way ahead of its time. Few pre-war manufacturers gave any thought to aerodynamic efficiency in their designs – in fact, streamlining wouldn't become a prime consideration in car design till the 1970s, when fuel price hikes made improving aerodynamic efficiency a priority in order to reduce fuel consumption. Put a 1930s' Beetle next to its contemporaries – cars like the 8hp Morris, Ford and Standard models, with their tall, upright bodywork and slab-like radiators – and it looks at least a generation younger.

This had one big advantage in that when production of the Beetle got seriously underway a decade later, its design had hardly dated. And as we know, the bodywork of the Beetle was to remain largely untouched for years to come.

Under the skin, however, a host of changes took place. The Beetle that was resurrected in 1945 was an austerely practical and unrefined vehicle that needed many improvements before it could become a serious force on the international motoring scene.

THE 1945 BEETLE

Because those immediate postwar Beetles were turned out in somewhat chaotic conditions, they didn't all necessarily share the same specification. However, in order to understand the changes that were made to the Beetle over the following decades, it's worth taking a good look at the design of a typical 1945 Beetle.

Bodywork, engine, transmission, brakes

Beetle 1200 Deluxe (1949–53)

Engine

Type	Air-cooled ohv flat-four, single-port cylinder heads
Capacity	1,131cc
Bore × stroke	75mm × 64mm
Compression ratio	5.8:1
Max. power	25bhp @ 3,300rpm
Max. torque	51lb/ft @ 2,000rpm

Transmission

Gearbox	Manual four-speed, with synchro on second, third and fourth
Gear ratios	1st: 3.60
	2nd: 1.88
	3rd: 1.23
	4th: 0.79
	Reverse: 4.63
	Final drive: 4.43

Suspension

Front	Independent with transverse torsion bars and trailing arms
Rear	Independent with swing axles, transverse torsion bars and trailing arms

Steering   Worm and nut

Brakes   Drum all-round, cable-operated (hydraulic from April 1950)

Dimensions (in/mm)

Length	160/4,070
Width	60/1,540
Weight	1,610lb (730kg)

Performance

0–50mph	24sec
30–50mph (in top gear)	27sec
Top speed	63mph (100km/h)
Fuel consumption	37mpg (7.6l/100km)

and suspension are all substantially true to Ferdinand Porsche's design. The body is bolted to a platform chassis which has a backbone running down its centre to give extra strength. There's a rubber seal between body and chassis which helps make the car pretty water-tight – as anyone unfortunate enough to drive a Beetle into a river was relieved to discover, there was generally plenty of time to get out and swim for shore before the 'Beetle-boat' became a 'Beetle-submarine'.

The sills are sealed square tubes that ingeniously double as heater channels, feeding warm air from exhaust heater boxes in the engine bay to the cabin, where heated air enters through outlets in the front footwells.

Air is drawn into the engine bay through a line of 42 vertical louvres cut into the bodywork immediately below the rear window. This window comprises a pair of kidney-shaped panes of flat glass, separated by a narrow bar – the famous 'split-screen'. The front windscreen is also a flat glass pane, with a pair of spindly windscreen wipers resting at its base (due to early post-war shortages, many cars had to make do with just one wiper, in front of the driver).

Front bonnet and rear engine lid are both opened by turning handles. Next to the opening handle at the rear is an aperture, into which a starting handle can be inserted should it be necessary to crank the engine by hand (which hopefully won't be necessary, as even the 1945 model has an electric starter motor).

Open the front bonnet, and there's a luggage compartment largely filled by an inconvenient rectangular fuel tank. In front of this sits the spare wheel, resting upright in its own well, and taking up its own hefty chunk of space. A comparatively small area remains for luggage. However, extra storage space is provided behind the rear seat.

There's a bulbous light pod on the engine lid, affectionately known as the 'pope's nose'. This provides both a stop light and number plate illumination. There are also two tiny rear lights mounted on the rear wings. Up front are a pair of sloping headlamps, which, being powered by the Beetle's six-volt electrical system, give an illumination easily matched by a couple of glow-worms. The battery lives under the rear seat. Semaphore indicators are built into the B-posts behind the front doors, and these are operated electrically by a switch on the dashboard.

At this stage the bodywork isn't much to look at – it's finished in matt paint, with painted hub caps and bumpers. Inside it's a similar story. Seats are basic and functional – early drivers were lucky to get any form of seat covering, and had to make do with an army greatcoat stretched over the seat frame. The seats are adjustable, however, by loosening wingnuts in the seat runners and sliding them backwards and forwards. A headlining is unlikely to be fitted, due to shortages of cloth. There is, however, a large courtesy light provided above the rear bench seat.

Instrumentation is kept to a bare minimum, with the painted steel dashboard adorned simply by a speedometer, graduated to 120km/h (75mph). No fuel gauge is fitted – the procedure is for the driver to wait till the car starts to splutter because it's running out of fuel, and then kick the fuel tap that opens the flow from the one-gallon reserve tank. This manoeuvre involves a little contortionism, because this tap is located in the passenger footwell.

In the driver's footwell is a headlamp dip switch, next to the accelerator (a tiny roller rather than a conventional flat pedal), and brake and clutch pedals (both of which sprout upwards from the floor). The handbrake is the usual ratchet lever, mounted on top of the tunnel formed by the chassis backbone, and immediately in front of it sits the gear lever. There's a manual choke fitted, and choke, accelerator and clutch cables are all neatly routed rearwards through the chassis tunnel (where they're a pig to replace when they snap).

Unlike pre-war Beetles which were fitted with 985cc engines, the 1945 car has the 1,131cc unit originally used in wartime Kübel and Schwimmwagens. Cooling is taken care of by an oil-cooler, and by the large engine fan which turns at twice engine speed and sucks in cool air through the louvres in the bodywork above the engine lid.

An engine built to last

The heart of the Beetle, its air-cooled flat-four engine, gained a remarkable reputation for ruggedness and reliability. Originally designed by Franz Reimspeiss specifically for the Beetle, it turned out to be a versatile unit. Over the years it has been put to an extraordinary range of uses, powering aeroplanes, speed boats, and factory machinery, as well as a whole range of vehicles from delivery vans to single-seater racing cars. However, poor Reimspeiss (who also gets the credit for creating the VW logo) received a bonus of less than £10 for designing it.

The Beetle's faithful flat-four was destined to grow from 985cc in the wartime Kübelwagen to 1,584cc in the current Mexican Beetle. It's always been noted for its relaxed, low-revving and long-lived nature.

From an original capacity of 985cc in the KdF-Wagen, the flat-four grew in a number of stages to 1,584cc in the 1303S, and more than doubled its power output in the process. Fuel injection was fitted to the later US-spec cars, as well as to the current Mexican model. Even a diesel variation was considered – prototypes were built in the early 1950s, and although this engine proved very economical, returning over 50mpg (5.6l/100km), Nordhoff considered it to be too noisy and unrefined to appeal to Beetle buyers.

Reimspeiss's main aims when he designed the engine were to make it simple, compact and lightweight. Simplicity was achieved by using air-cooling, which dispensed with the need for a radiator and removed the problem of the coolant freezing in winter or boiling over in summer.

Short dimensions and light weight were both vital in view of the engine's position, slung out behind the rear wheels. The heavier and longer the engine, the greater the polar moment of inertia of the car would be, and the less stable its handling.

Adopting a flat-four configuration, with twin horizontally opposed banks of two cylinders, kept the engine sufficiently short and made it naturally well-balanced as well. A low weight was achieved by the extensive use of light metals such as magnesium. These were more expensive than conventional materials, but the vast scale of Beetle production made it economical to use them. By the late 1960s VW had become the biggest consumer of magnesium, using 30,000 tonnes annually, one-fifth of total world production.

The Beetle's engine was designed for dependability and economy, not outright power. In its original 985cc guise it was considered to be underpowered for use in wartime VWs. It duly received its first hike in capacity, to 1,131cc, and it was in this form that it was fitted to the first postwar Beetles. Even by the standards of the 1940s, its output of 22bhp per litre was nothing to brag about. What did make the engine special was its sheer unburstability. As *Autocar* explained, in relation to the later 1,285cc version of the flat-four:

> An unusual characteristic of the Volkswagen engine is its breathing restriction at the top end – this is undoubtedly one of the secrets of its long life. It is a unit which can never be over-driven because at 4,500rpm, or thereabouts, the induction pipes are passing their maximum flow of mixture, and any higher revs take so long to reach that performance suffers if the driver doesn't change up. We managed to run beyond 6,000rpm to record 27mph in first, but this entailed driving some distance flat out in bottom just to see what happened.

As the years passed there was an increasing need to extract more power from the engine to keep up with the ever-improving performance of newer models coming onto the marketplace. These demands for more power were met by increasing the capacity of the engine, improving its breathing and raising its compression ratio. From a starting point of 5.6:1 on the first Beetles (which made them so indifferent to fuel quality that, as one journalist quipped, you could practically run them on water), compression ratios increased to 7.5:1 on the 1300 and 1600 engines fitted to the Super Beetles.

All this extra performance put a strain on the flat-four it had never been intended to cope with. Later, larger capacity versions of the engine, while not being unreliable, certainly didn't merit the reputation for indestructibility that their predecessors had earned. One step that particularly weakened the engine was fitting the twin inlet-port cylinder heads of the Super Beetle models. They increased power output by allowing the engine to breathe more efficiently, but the new heads proved to be prone to developing cracks between the inlet ports.

At the same time, the emissions control equipment that had to be fitted in the US was sapping the Beetle engine of its power. The ultimate increase in capacity from 1,493cc to 1,584cc, was needed largely to compensate for the loss in performance on the American market.

Since Beetles have ceased to be made in Europe, development of the flat-four has continued in Mexico and Brazil. One particularly interesting Brazilian modification allows the engine to run on alcohol, cheaply distilled from the sugar cane which grows there in abundance. The current 1,584cc alcohol-powered Beetle runs a compression ratio of 11:1, produces 59bhp at 4,300rpm, dispatches the 0–60mph (100km/h) dash in around fifteen seconds, and covers some 27 miles for every gallon of alcohol it drinks (10.4l/100km).

Meanwhile, in Mexico, today's flat-four has come a long way from the original design sketched out by Franz Reimspeiss. The 1600 unit boasts maintenance-free hydraulic tappets, twin-port cylinder heads, a proper oil filter and multi-point electronic fuel injection. The fuel injection system, according to a recent VW de Mexico sales brochure, represents the ultimate improvement to the Beetle's venerable engine, 'like dotting the "i" or putting the icing on the cake'.

Early cars featured a tiny roller accelerator pedal – this was replaced by the organ type in 1957.

The engine feeds its 25bhp to the rear wheels via a four-speed gearbox, which at this stage is not equipped with synchromesh. Drive from the gearbox to the rear wheels is transmitted by swinging half axles enclosed in cylindrical tubes. Suspension is by Porsche-patented torsion bars all-round, and steering is a worm-and-nut system. Braking front and rear is taken care of by cable-operated drums, and the handbrake on these early cars works, very effectively, on all four wheels.

This, then, is the Beetle which started to roll off the production lines after the five-year hiatus of war. Food and raw material shortages hindered production, but the demand for transport from the occupying forces made getting cars built a matter of urgency. The Beetle at this stage still had many rough edges to its design, and the grim working conditions at the factory meant that its finish and detailing were cruder still.

MINOR IMPROVEMENTS

There was little time to spare to start putting right these defects, but even so the factory managed to attend to some items over the next three years, until Heinrich Nordhoff arrived on the scene in 1948 and started paying serious attention to improving quality.

One bugbear that was to remain a problem for several years to come was excessive noise. Air-cooled engines are naturally louder than water-cooled ones, and the

111

Although the Beetle retained its traditional torsion bar front suspension for many years, Volkswagen kept tinkering with the number of leaves in each bar to get the best ride/handling compromise – these are five-leaf springs, fitted from 1950–53.

clamour of the Beetle's poorly insulated flat-four reverberated round a cabin which had little in the way of soft material to soak up the decibels. Stiff cardboard was fitted in the engine bay and this went some way to deadening the racket.

There had also been a problem with cars falling off their jacks when they were raised off the ground. This was cured by modifying the jacking points welded under the sills, making them square instead of round.

Apart from these minor changes, the Beetle soldiered on much the same during the years of the British occupation, basically sound but unpolished. In those days, of course, Beetles were still hard to get hold

of, and only tentative efforts were made to export them. However, in 1947 the magazine *Motor* managed to test a Beetle brought home by an RAF officer on leave.

The impression it made was generally a favourable one. 'It is difficult to think of any car in the popular priced class which is in more striking contrast to current British models,' said *Motor's* tester, who was impressed by the slickness of the car's 'delightful' gearbox, despite the lack of synchromesh to aid smooth changing. Ride and handling came in for praise, although a lack of refinement was noted. 'In town, it must be said that the car is noisy by 1947 standards, with a good deal of gear hum in third or fourth speeds and more distinct noise in the lower ratio.' However, 'on the open road, the overdrive top gear provides immensely effortless cruising'. Overall, the Beetle appeared to be 'a sound job which should give long years of service with the minimum of professional attention'.

In 1949 came a fresh direction for the Beetle. Under Nordhoff's leadership conditions at Wolfsburg were more settled, a concerted effort was made to improve quality and three glamorous new models were launched – the Cabriolets from Hebmüller and Karmann, and the Deluxe or Export version of the saloon.

EXPORT MODELS

Designed to launch the Beetle onto the world stage, the Export model boasted smart gloss paintwork in Bordeaux-red, mid-brown, pastel-green or gloss black, alloy strips along its waistline, running boards and the centre of its bonnet, and chrome-plated hubcaps, bumpers, door handles and headlamp rims. Inside, the Export was far more attractively laid out than the standard model, with smart cloth upholstery, easily adjustable seats, an attractively styled two-spoke steering wheel and a brightly-finished dashboard. The front seats received spring-loaded handles in the place of the old wing nuts, allowing easier fore-and-aft adjustment.

For the first time a VW emblem was placed on the bonnet. A cable release now allowed this bonnet to be opened from inside the car, so the turning handle on the bonnet was replaced by a simple grab handle. Due to the repositioning of the horn under the left front wing, a hole covered with a circular chromed grille was added beneath the headlamp, and a dummy grille was fitted on the right-hand side to match

it. The hole in the engine lid for the starting handle, meanwhile, was deleted. These refinements also found their way onto the cabriolet models, which throughout their lives were trimmed to Export standard.

The split of the Beetle saloon range into Export and standard models established a tradition that was to last for many years. Innovations invariably featured on the Export model long before they found their way onto the standard car, which retained a starkly utilitarian outlook. The benefit for the standard saloon in doing so was, of course, that it could be sold much more cheaply: when it was made available in the UK in 1967, a standard Beetle cost £586, £75 less than the Export-spec 1300. Unless specified, the modifications to the Beetle mentioned in the following pages apply to the Export model, not necessarily to the standard Beetle as well.

MODIFICATIONS

Alongside the cosmetic changes made in 1949 came minor, but important, modifications to the engine, transmission and suspension aimed at improving reliability. Tougher exhaust valves were fitted, along with a more efficient air filter. The cylinder barrels were strengthened by upping their phosphor content, while the gearbox casing material changed to a magnesium alloy known as Elektron. Better insulation cut down the degree of engine noise in the cabin. On the front suspension, single-acting shock absorbers were replaced by more efficient double-acting ones.

In 1950 the pace of improvement was kept up. The design of the engine air filter was changed for the second year running, and extra sound-proofing around the heater pipes helped reduce the still intrusive level of engine noise.

Extra sound-proofing was placed around the heater pipes under the rear seats in 1950 as part of a continuing effort to reduce the high noise levels inside early Beetles.

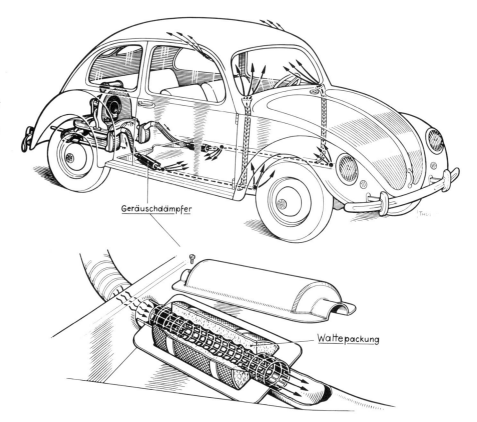

Geräuschdämpfer

Wattepackung

Several attempts were made to improve ventilation inside early Beetles – the notch in the front side window panes and opening flaps on the front quarter panels of this 1951 car were both short-lived measures.

An extra leaf was added to the upper torsion bar on the front suspension, giving a slightly firmer ride. Hydraulic brakes were introduced, with a master cylinder and fluid reservoir below the petrol tank. The standard model soldiered on with cable brakes for another fourteen years, though.

The first in a continuing series of attempts to improve ventilation came in the form of nicks cut out of the top corners of the front door windows, a Heath-Robinsonish modification which allowed a draught-free flow of air to enter the cabin. For even better ventilation, there was the option of ordering at extra cost opening rear side windows, or, more enticingly, a sliding canvas sun roof.

The engine crankcase was strengthened in 1951, when it was cast in Elektron. Around the same time the rear suspension received double-acting shock-absorbers to match those at the front.

Another stab was made at improving ventilation, with opening flaps placed in the front quarter panels and operated by levers in the cabin. In practice, these proved difficult to adjust to give precisely the degree of air flow required – back to the drawing board on that one.

The bodywork received a couple of embellishing features – a chromed windscreen surround and an ornate enamel badge on the bonnet. This, rather ironically, featured part of the coat of arms of Count von der Schulenburg, the aristocratic owner of the Wolfsburg estate who had tried so hard to stop the factory being built there in the first place.

By this stage, thanks to the numerous detail improvements that had been made, the Beetle had become a well-proven design with a growing reputation for reliability. Nordhoff still wasn't entirely happy with it. With increasing production had come a series of inexplicable problems that reduced the longevity of some engines. 'In the end,' Nordhoff wryly recalled, 'to placate the gods, I promised a gold wristwatch and a personal testimony of gratitude to every driver who covered 100,000km with one and the same engine.'

The gods took notice, and owners

In the 1950s, more than 160,000 Beetle owners were presented with a watch and certificate for covering 100,000km on one engine. By 1961 reliability was so good that the scheme had to be scrapped.

responded eagerly to this initiative. In 1952, 2,000 100,000km Beetles gathered at the small German town of Erbach. Two years later 35,000 attended a similar rally in Stuttgart. By 1961, over 160,000 100,000km Beetles had been recognized, and VW, which was rapidly running out of wristwatches, decided to bring the scheme to an end.

Those whose engines hadn't lasted so well were also catered for. In an offer unique in the motor industry at the time, Volkswagen offered complete exchange engines at less than half the price of a new engine – so successful was this policy that by 1958 one out of every ten Beetles was running on a replacement engine.

Despite the considerable improvements it had made to the Beetle, Volkswagen refused to rest on its laurels. In 1952 a whole host of changes was made. This year also saw the first factory-built right-hand-drive Beetle heading for the UK.

In came opening quarterlights in the front windows, replacing both the nick cut in the window glass and the vents in the front quarter panels. This at last was a reasonable response to the challenge of providing adequate ventilation. Extra chrome trim round the side and rear windows also distinguished the 1952 model, and eagle-eyed observers would have spotted that the round horn grilles under the headlamps had been made oval. Stop lights were added to the rear lights, though as this stop light sat on top of the housing it gave a clearer warning to passing aircraft than following traffic. The 'pope's nose' numberplate light housing was modified, and the handle on the engine lid became T-shaped.

Later in the year some striking improvements were made inside, with a neat new dashboard featuring a lidded glovebox, ashtray, provision for a radio and speaker and a large speedometer directly in front of the driver. Within the speedo dial were situated handy warning lights for ignition, oil pressure and headlight main beam. The central horn button on the two-spoke steering wheel was embellished by a gold-on-black Wolfsburg Castle emblem.

Running gear came in for some attention

Opening quarterlights were a better long-term solution to the problem of providing adequate ventilation – they appeared in 1952, replacing the notched side window and quarter panel ventilation flap of the previous year.

Tiny tail lights (left) were fitted until 1952, when larger ones replaced them (right). These also incorporated a stop lamp, but as this was fitted in the top of the housing it gave more warning to aeroplanes flying overhead than to following traffic.

In 1953 the split rear window was replaced with an oval window which gives slightly better visibility.

117

too. Carburettor modifications helped elim-
inate flat-spots, a sixth leaf was added to
both upper and lower torsion bars in the
front axle to improve ride comfort, and the
gearbox gained synchromesh on second,
third and fourth. The wheels were reduced
by one inch in diameter to fifteen inches.

The following year – 1953 – saw Beetle
sales begin properly in Britain. The 945
cars that were imported had one important
difference to the previous year's model – at
the rear of the body was a single oval window. This change, which forms one of the
relatively few obvious demarcation-points
in the evolution of the Beetle, arrived in
mid-March. Nowadays, of course, the small
number of split-window cars are all highly

cherished, but in the early 1950s many
owners were impressed by the extra visibility provided by the oval window design, and
proceeded to have their own cars modified.

Motor published a road test of one of
these UK Beetles on 1 April 1953, but as
befitting this august journal, it was a sober,
considered account. Their example
achieved a top speed of 62.8mph
(100.5km/h), accelerated from 30 to 50mph
(50 to 80km/h) in top gear in 27.5 seconds,
and covered the quarter mile in 24.6 seconds. Brisk performance was aided by the
slick gearbox, described as 'just about the
sweetest on any inexpensive car now made'.

Fuel consumption – at 37.1mpg
(7.6l/100km) overall – was also singled out

*There's precious little luggage space under the bonnet of a torsion bar Beetle – most of the room is
taken up by the fuel tank and spare wheel. Later Super Beetles, with MacPherson strut front
suspensions, have almost twice as much space under the front bonnet.*

as worthy of praise, and the ride, though firm, was considered comfortable. They commented on the suspension's ability to iron out rough surfaces tackled at speed – a feature which was also praised by Australian magazine *Wheels*, who drove a Beetle flat out along a corrugated gravel track and reported that 'riding comfort under this severe run was exceptional'.

Other modifications made included yet more fiddling with the front torsion bars, with the number of leaves increased to eight. The fuel filler neck was doubled in diameter to 80mm. Inside, the changes were minor: the steering-wheel spokes were modified to give a clearer view of the

---

Beetle 1200 Deluxe (1954–60)

Engine

Type	Air-cooled ohv flat-four, single-port cylinder heads
Capacity	1,192cc
Bore × stroke	77mm × 64mm
Compression ratio	6.6:1
Max. power	30bhp @ 3,400rpm
Max. torque	56lb/ft @ 2,000rpm

Transmission

Gearbox	Manual four-speed, with synchro on second, third and fourth
Gear ratios	1st: 3.60
	2nd: 1.88
	3rd: 1.23
	4th: 0.82
	Reverse: 4.63
	Final drive: 4.43

Suspension

Front	Independent with transverse torsion bars and trailing arms
Rear	Independent with swing axles, transverse torsion bars and trailing arms

Steering

Worm and nut

Brakes

Drum all-round

Dimensions (in/mm)

Length	160/4,070
Width	60/1,540
Weight	1,610lb (730kg)

Performance

0–50mph	20sec
30–50mph (top gear)	24sec
Top speed	66mph (105km/h)
Fuel consumption	35mpg (8.0l/100km)

speedo, and the front quarterlights gained push-buttons.

There were some other important changes in 1953, but they arrived so late in the year (on 21 December to be precise) that they really only applied to 1954 models.

The biggest change came to the engine. The 1,131cc 25bhp unit which had been used since the relaunch of the Beetle in 1945 was bored out to give a capacity of 1,192cc. Combined with an increase in the compression ratio from 5.8:1 to 6.1:1, this liberated an extra 5bhp, which may not sound much, but as it represented an increase of twenty per cent over the old engine, it made for a noticeable improvement to the Beetle's performance.

Motor, testing the latest 1,192cc oval-window Export Beetle, recorded a top speed of 66.1mph (105.8km/h), 3mph quicker than the 1953 model. More impressive was the 30 to 50mph (50 to 80km/h) acceleration time in top gear – the torquier new engine shaved off over five seconds to return a time of 22.3 seconds. *Motor* was not overly impressed, though, calling the Beetle's 30bhp 'still a very modest output for a 1.2-litre engine'.

Despite the performance gains, fuel consumption remained frugal; *Motor* achieved 34.5mpg (8.7l/100km) overall, and 39.6mpg (7.1l/100km) on an easy run. 'The very high top gear of this VW pays handsome dividends in fuel economy where main road touring is concerned.'

One significant point was made about the Beetle's top speed:

> Whereas, with most cars, maximum is regarded as an ultimate to be reached on occasions but not normally to be held for long periods of continuous running, the maximum of the VW is not only approved by its manufacturers as a cruising speed, but is even sanctioned for running-in!

This point was graphically illustrated by one competitor in the 1954 RAC Rally, who entered a brand new Beetle and happily proceeded to drive flat out for more than 2,000 miles. That would have been a sure recipe for disaster in any other car of the time, but the Beetle soaked it up, returning 35mpg (8.1l/100km) over the course of the rally, and using less than a pint of oil.

Motor did point out one drawback of the Beetle's unusually high top gear ratio which allowed endless flat-out motoring:

> The manufacturers have made no compromise in the choice of top-gear ratio in the interests of flexibility, and top gear remains – in mechanical fact as well as in effect – an overdrive ratio which is excellent for main-road running but less appropriate in town or in winding lanes. In consequence, once trunk roads are left, the VW owner has to be prepared to make frequent use of the gear lever and, indeed, to employ third very extensively (but) this cannot be regarded as a penance thanks to the very handily-placed central lever and the excellence of the synchromesh.
>
> Although air-cooled, the engine is reasonably quiet mechanically, and appears even more so to people actually inside the car owing to its rear disposition, but there is some whine from the shrouded cooling fan and this, in conjunction with a far-from-silent transmission in which torque reversals as well as gear hum are audible at low speeds, makes the VW less quiet than the normal run of small cars.

Also noted was the tendency of the Beetle's weighty tail to swing out when cornering hard:

> Within normal limits, cornering is outstandingly good. If, however, the limit of discretion is exceeded on a corner, a sharp

oversteer tendency develops very suddenly indeed, calling for instant correction on the steering. Only the more exuberant of drivers are liable to experience this peculiarity at all frequently, and such drivers are not likely to find any difficulty in dealing with it when it does arise.

Motor concluded that the Beetle, then priced £689 12s 6d, 'undoubtedly justifies its aim as a people's car and has very considerable appeal to the enthusiast as well.'

Despite a hectic start to the year, VW found time to make a few more detail improvements to the Beetle in 1954 – higher quality seat fabrics were introduced, rubber foot pads were added to the brake and clutch pedals, the brake fluid reservoir was moved to a more accessible location behind the spare wheel, the interior courtesy light was relocated above the passenger door and

came on whenever a door was opened, and the push-button starter was replaced by a key-operated switch on the dashboard.

US models received larger combined rear and stop lights, but this useful modification didn't reach European markets until the following year – the start of an increasing trend for changes, particularly safety-related ones, to appear first on cars destined for America. This was seen again in 1955, when US-spec Beetles received flashing direction indicators built into the front wings, while European ones kept the old semaphore indicators till 1960. US cars were also equipped with bigger bumpers.

This year also saw Volkswagen adopt an August-to-August production year. Instead of introducing updates at irregular periods during the year, changes were lumped together and the production line machinery altered during the August factory

The millionth Beetle arrived in 1955. Ten years later a million Beetles were being built each year.

break. Thus changes made in 1955 were applied to cars produced in the 1956 model year, which ran from August 1955 to August 1956.

The 1955 modifications also included a reshaped fuel tank, which gave a marginal increase in luggage space, and the fuel filler neck, enlarged in diameter from 40 to 80mm in 1953, was now reduced to 60mm.

The heater control knob was moved to a more convenient location further forward on the chassis tunnel, and the gear lever had to be given a pronounced crank so as not to foul it. Front seat backrests were made adjustable to three settings. The single exhaust outlet was replaced by twin chromed pipes.

Few changes were made the following year, other than strengthening the camshaft timing gear, which had been proving unreliable, and fitting tubeless (but still cross-ply) tyres.

By now the Beetle was rapidly increas-

ing in popularity, much to the surprise of some motoring commentators. Writing in *Autosport,* John Bolster remarked that:

> The phenomenal success of the Volkswagen is, to many, one of the greatest surprises of the age. It lacks the superficial attraction of some of its competitors – indeed, the separate mud-guards joined by running boards, the shallow screen and blind rear quarters, all serve to emphasize that this is a pre-war design. Yet the Volkswagen goes from strength to strength.

Motor, too, picked up on the paradox of the Beetle, asking:

> What are the characteristics in the design and performance of the car which make many of the million and more buyers almost passionate in the defence of their choice and, almost equally important, why do a number of professional engineers and

One of the last oval window Beetles. By 1957, quality control had improved immensely at Wolfburg and the Beetle was gaining a strong reputation for its fine standard of finish, build integrity and reliability.

journalists take the view that the car is crude in design, mediocre in performance, and difficult, or even dangerous, to drive?

There was clearly something in the appeal of the Beetle that couldn't be summed up adequately in the dry, objective, terms of the traditional magazine road test. Buyers, however, appreciated the Beetle's hidden charms, queued up to drive it away, and enthusiastically spread the word to win yet more converts to the cause. Volkswagen's best advertisement came free, in the loyalty and support of its customers, who championed the Beetle with an enthusiasm that made it the envy of other motor manufacturers.

7 An Expanding Range: 1300 and 1500

By Volkswagen's standards, 1957 marked a major facelift for the Beetle. In fact, the changes were relatively minor, but they made these and later Beetles instantly distinguishable from those that had gone before.

Much criticism had been fired at the Beetle's poor visibility – the small front and rear screens were an obvious hangover from its pre-war origins, and a source of concern to buyers accustomed to the larger glass areas of more modern designs. Accordingly, the bodywork of the 1957 was restyled to improve visibility. Out went the

Beetles never looked the same again after the rectangular rear screen was introduced in 1957, almost doubling rear visibility. It increased slightly in size once more (as pictured) in 1964, and yet again in 1971. The front windscreen also grew and grew over the years.

oval rear screen, to be replaced by a rectangular screen nearly twice the size – at the same time the front windscreen was enlarged (though it still consisted of a flat pane of glass). As a consequence of the increased glass area, the engine air intake louvres had to be reduced in size, and a simpler engine lid design was introduced.

Whether these changes were for better or worse depends on your perspective. To the modern enthusiast, the larger screens detract from the balance and purity of line of the original Beetle. To the average buyer in 1957, they were very much a step forward. The new Beetle was lighter, airier and generally more pleasant inside, and its improved visibility made it safer and easier to drive.

The interior received an update too, with a more modern dashboard that featured a larger glovebox, a bigger rear-view mirror and a flat organ-type throttle pedal in place of the roller-ball original. At the same time, an extra helping of sound-proofing material made driving a Beetle a more relaxing experience.

New colours arrived – glacier blue, light bronze, diamond grey and Capri for the saloon, and alabaster, atlas blue, Shetland grey and bamboo for the Cabriolet.

As buyers had by now come to expect from Volkswagen, build quality was impec-

For 1958 the Beetle received a new dashboard, with a larger glovebox and more conveniently arranged switchgear. The radio moved to the middle of the dashboard, with a speaker installed beside the speedometer. Extra soundproofing meant you could hear the radio better too.

cable. *Autocar*, testing the big window Beetle, commented:

> The standard of the finish is exceptionally high for a car in this price class. From the paintwork to such details as the fit of the glove locker lid, the car earns commendation.
>
> The Volkswagen appeal is widely based and the ex-works price and running costs are particularly modest. A sporting driver will like it for the precision of its controls, even though the acceleration is below modern standards for the size of car. It is equally at home on long straight motor roads or mountain passes. The restful nature of its progress and the ease of control will appeal to the older or quieter driver – the traction and the way in which it copes with very rough surfaces clearly have an appeal for farmers and others whose driving is undertaken over rough tracks and mud.

COMPETITORS

After carrying out such a comprehensive facelift, Wolfsburg took a brief rest and made only a handful of minor alterations to the Beetle in 1958. As the swelling ranks of Beetle owners proved, the formula was working well enough as it was. *Wheels* ran a head-to-head test against Triumph's brand new Herald. As the introduction suggested – 'Bravely, the ageing Beetle meets Britain's boldest bid in 20 years' – Volkswagen's offering should logically have been outclassed by this newcomer with all the force of modern technology behind it.

Wheels' conclusion told a different story. 'Which will most people buy? Frankly, we cannot say. Never has there been a pair of cars so similarly priced, so utterly brilliant in conception and yet with so little to choose between them.' Hard to imagine a similar conclusion being reached by one of today's motoring magazines after testing a brand new model against one that first saw the light of day twenty years ago.

If Triumph had cause to be worried by the Beetle's continuing display of abilities, they weren't alone. Ford had launched the Anglia at the 1959 Earl's Court Motor Show, and soon afterwards issued its sales staff with a pamphlet giving advice to them on how to convince buyers to buy an Anglia, and not a Beetle from the VW dealership down the road.

Ford ruefully mentions in this pamphlet how the Beetle 'has something about it which makes the million and more owners rise fanatically in its defence'. VW owners are, it admits, converted into enthusiastic publicity agents, and 'we know that many people buy VWs mainly because of the high praise showered upon the cars by fellow owners'. However, it urged that sales staff should take heart from the engineers and journalists who hold the view that the Beetle is 'not only crude in design and mediocre in performance, but difficult and even dangerous to drive'.

The pamphlet recommended that Ford sales staff should point out the Beetle's drawbacks: that much time must be spent in its noisy third gear, as its high-geared fourth ratio is unsuitable for driving conditions in the UK (where there were then only 75 miles (120km) of motorway); that the Beetle is prone to oversteer, especially with just the driver on board; that it has a serious lack of luggage space; that its heater is ineffective and prone to blowing oil fumes into the cabin; that few colours are available (seven against the Anglia's eleven); and that the headlining inside the Beetle (you can imagine a rising note of desperation in the voice of any salesman who had to dredge this far down the list to convince a customer) was made from a non-washable cloth.

Presumably a VW salesman could have come straight back with a list of similar drawbacks to the Ford Anglia, but in the main these criticisms were valid. Volkswagen did recognize its car's failings, however, and over the coming years took measures to combat them.

1960 MODEL

Already, for the 1960 model year, steps had been taken to tame the Beetle's oversteer. An anti-roll bar was fitted to the front sus-

---

A sting in the tail

Back in the mid-1930s when Ferdinand Porsche designed the Beetle, putting the engine at the rear end of the body made a lot of sense. It avoided the need for a heavy, expensive propshaft to connect a front engine to rear driven wheels, it saved space in the passenger cabin and, by putting the weight of the engine directly over the driven wheels, it gave them better traction in really slippery conditions.

But a rear-engined design brought with it its own set of problems. When driven really quickly around a corner so that the sideways force acting on the car starts to overcome the grip exerted by its tyres, a rear-engined car tends to be harder to control and less predictable in its handling than one with the engine out front.

If it is driven round a corner too quickly, a front-engined car naturally understeers. That is, the front of the car moves outwards, increasing the radius of the turn. When this happens, the natural, instinctive, reaction of most drivers is to lift off the throttle or even brake. In most cases, the slight loss of speed this causes allows the front tyres to regain their grip, cancels out the understeer, and the car returns to its original course. Essentially it's a very safe handling characteristic, and it means that drivers don't need any special skill or experience to be able to regain control if they take a corner too fast.

A rear-engined car like the Beetle also understeers in most conditions. But because its weight is concentrated in the rear, there are circumstances under which it will try to oversteer instead. That means the rear of the car slides outwards, decreasing the radius of the turn and ultimately causing the car to spin. Oversteer is most likely to occur if the driver lifts off the throttle or applies the brakes while cornering hard, because doing this transfers the weight of the car forwards, reducing the traction of the rear wheels.

Early Beetles are particularly prone to oversteer, and this characteristic is exacerbated by their simple swing-axle rear suspension. This allows the rear camber (the angle that the wheels make against the road surface) to alter depending on the forces acting on the suspension. Lift off while cornering fast in an early Beetle, and the rear wheels will jack up and lean over, reducing the area of contact between tyre tread and tarmac.

This tricky handling trait didn't seem so important when the first Beetles were built. Cars were generally more difficult to drive then, with crash gearboxes, heavy brakes, skinny tyres and vague steering. Road surfaces were also poorer, but drivers were fewer in number and it was assumed they would possess the skill to deal with the challenges that driving presented.

In skilled hands, an early Beetle doesn't pose a problem. The reverse can be the case: enthusiastic drivers have always enjoyed the ease with which a Beetle can be flicked round corners with a controlled measure of oversteer. But as the years passed, driving became more widely practised, suspensions and tyres improved, and the average driver no longer acquired the range of skills that were needed in the early days of motoring. It was then that the Beetle began to be labelled as a car that didn't handle safely.

Who says Beetles don't handle! The Beetle's oversteering characteristic may have come in for criticism over the years, but in skilled hands it can be used to good advantage.

Not that the Beetle was alone in deserving this criticism – as anyone who's ever driven a (front-engined, but also swing-axled) Triumph Herald or GT6 will know. What brought the issue to a head was a campaign against rear-engined cars orchestrated by Ralph Nader in the US. Nader, a lawyer, focused the main thrust of his attack on the Chevrolet Corvair in his book *Unsafe at Any Speed*. Later he turned his attention to the Beetle in another book, *Volkswagen: Small on Safety*. VW vigorously refuted Nader's claims, having already taken several steps to curb the tail-happy nature of the Beetle, but there's no doubt that they responded to the climate engendered by Nader's campaign by becoming much more safety-conscious.

Volkswagen's first attempt to improve the Beetle's handling came in 1959, when a front anti-roll bar was fitted and the pivot point of the rear swing axles lowered by tilting the engine and gearbox forward by two degrees. This made the handling more neutral – though, interestingly, the successful Beetle rally driver Bill Bengry used to remove the anti-roll bar, insisting that his car could be driven more quickly without it.

The next improvement came in 1966, when an equalizer spring was fitted to the rear axle tubes. This gave extra support to the torsion bars when cornering hard, and vastly improved the road-holding abilities of the rear wheels. Criticism of the Beetle's handling markedly declined after this modification, although genuinely foolproof handling only arrived with the double-jointed rear axle which arrived with the semi-automatic Beetle in 1967. This was more expensive than the existing set-up (which was why VW took so long to extend it to the rest of the range) but it banished forever the problem of the rear wheels jacking up.

On the other hand, as far as some enthusiasts are concerned this measure pushed the handling balance too far in the other direction, and the old swing-axle system is to be preferred for its more satisfying and responsive handling. There is, after all, nothing to beat the rear-engined layout if you enjoy enthusiastic driving – just ask any Porsche 911 owner.

This 1947 Beetle was one of the very first cars converted to a higher specification and sold in the UK. Dealer John Colborne-Baber added the two-tone paint scheme and chromed trim.

The split rear window is an unmistakeable feature of an early Beetle.

For obvious reasons the numberplate light housing was nicknamed the 'Pope's nose'.

The air-cooled flat-four Beetle engine has a fine reliability record; this 30bhp example has covered 270,000 miles (435,000km) without a rebuild.

This 1956 1200 well displays the classic lines and balanced proportions of the Beetle design.

US-spec Beetles had flashing indicators from 1955 but British cars continued with semaphores until 1960.

The badging on early Beetles depicts Wolfsburg Castle, part of the coat of arms of the aristocrat who tried to prevent VW building the Beetle factory on his land.

'Eyelids' were a popular character accessory, but they were outlawed as a danger to pedestrians in the Beetle's native Germany.

The optional tool kit fits neatly within the spare wheel.

This 1970 1300 Beetle features attractive older style cream-painted wheels.

The painted metal dashboard gives the car an uncluttered appearance.

The crescent-shaped air vent was introduced in 1970 as one of the repeated attempts to improve Beetle ventilation.

The trigger-release door handle was one of many safety features introduced in 1967.

Glovebox showing the bonnet release lever.

The 1985 Jubilee special edition looks superb with elegant pewter-grey paintwork and tinted glass. This is one of the last Mexican cars officially imported to Europe.

The Jubilee interior shows how far things had come from the austerity of the first models.

Mexican cars continued to use pre-Super Beetle bodyshell and torsion-bar front suspension, but featured 1303 rear lamp clusters.

Cabriolets were based on the 1303 Super Beetle bodyshell until production ceased in 1980.

The heavy-duty hood keeps out road noise and draughts and the proper glass screen gives decent rear visibility.

Late cabriolets like this 1979 US-spec model had luxurious interiors including walnut-effect dashboard.

pension, while at the rear, the pivot points of the swing axles were lowered by tilting the engine slightly forwards. This was a partial solution – further measures would later be required as the driving public became accustomed to increasingly fool-proof handling from their cars.

Along with these modifications came the usual annual batch of Beetle improvements. On the outside, push-button safety door handles were fitted. Inside, yet more sound-proofing was added, and heelboard panels blanked off the area beneath the rear seat, cutting down engine noise as well as tidying up the interior. The steering wheel was modified slightly to include a half-circle chrome horn ring, the front seats were redesigned to fit the curve of the spine better, and front-seat passengers gained a black-painted metal foot rest.

1961 MODEL

For the 1961 model year, VW decided it was time to introduce more substantial changes. The Beetle received a significantly revised engine and transmission – a combination which had already been tried and tested in the Type 2 Transporter since May 1959.

Although still 1,192cc in capacity, the internals of the engine had been thoroughly reworked, and its compression ratio was increased from 6.6:1 to 7.0:1. This raised the power output from 30 to 34bhp. A slower-rotating cooling fan also made the new engine a little quieter.

With this engine came a switch to an automatic choke – fitted, it seems, because some owners were leaving the manual choke on for too long, causing the cylinders to flood with petrol which washed away the protective coat of lubricating oil, and over time led to excessive bore wear. Cold run-

ning was also improved by feeding air from the heat exchangers into the carburettor, a modification which helped stop the carburettor icing up in cold weather, a common Beetle malady.

The transmission now featured synchromesh on all four forward gears, and it had a revised set of ratios that gave better acceleration on the open road.

Meanwhile, a steering damper was fitted, the fusebox was moved inside the car beneath the dashboard, a passenger grab handle was fitted to the dashboard and, at long last, flashing indicators replaced semaphores on European models. These were housed in chrome-plated pods mounted on top of the front wings, and incorporated in the stop/rear light pods at the back.

Autocar received the new Beetle enthusiastically, declaring:

> Every time one renews acquaintance with the VW, the first reaction is admiration at a standard of finish without equal among the world's mass-produced cars. Not only is the body presswork practically without flaw and the paint finish smooth and lustrous, but the finish bears close scrutiny even in such usually untidy areas as around the door hinges. Inside the body the only screw heads visible are three securing the rear-view mirror bracket and one in each sun visor. A typical detail is that the ashtray in the facia slides on four little brass rollers.

The magazine found real improvements in performance, and cracked the 70mph (110km/h) barrier to achieve a top speed of 72mph (115km/h). From a standing start 50mph (80km/h) came up in 17.7sec, compared with 22.4sec for the 30bhp car *Autocar* had tested three years before. More importantly, the time taken to accelerate from 30 to 50mph (50–80km/h) in top

Beetle 1200 Deluxe (1960–78)

Engine
Type	Air-cooled ohv flat-four, single-port cylinder heads
Capacity	1,192cc
Bore × stroke	77mm × 64mm
Compression ratio	7.0:1
Max. power	34bhp @ 3,600rpm
Max. torque	61lb/ft @ 2,000rpm

Transmission
Gearbox	Manual four-speed, synchro on all forward gears
Gear ratios	1st: 3.80
	2nd: 2.06
	3rd: 1.32
	4th: 0.89
	Reverse: 3.88
	Final drive: 4.38

Suspension
Front	Independent with transverse torsion bars and trailing arms; anti-roll bar
Rear	Independent with swing axles, transverse torsion bars and trailing arms

Steering
Worm and roller

Brakes
Drum all-round

Dimensions (in/mm)
Length	160/4,070
Width	60/1,540
Weight	1,630lb (740kg)

Performance
0–60mph	28sec
30–50mph (top gear)	20sec
Top speed	71mph (114km/h)
Fuel consumption	34mpg (8.3l/100km)

was down from 22.6 to 18.0sec, which meant there was a lot less need for gearchanging on the open road. Despite this, VW made it clear that it was still quite safe to run the Beetle at maximum speed for hours on end, and even to allow extra speed to build up on downhill stretch-

es. Even at its maximum speed, the engine was turning at a leisurely 3,900rpm.

Autocar quibbled with the conservative maximum speeds recommended by VW in the lower gears – 15mph (24km/h) in first, 30 (48km/h) in second and 45 (72km/h) in third. 'If one were to adhere to these figures the VW's rate of progress would be very restricted.' *Autocar* thought 5,000rpm was a more reasonable limit – one that would allow 63mph to be achieved in third gear.

The new all-synchro gear box received top marks – 'The VW might well claim to have the best manual gearbox of any car' – but despite improvements to suspension and steering, it was felt that the Beetle's rear-engined handling characteristics still presented 'greater problems of acclimatization than a good front-drive design. At first one may be so disturbed at the sensation of "the tail trying to wag the dog" as to drive this car very gingerly round corners.'

Minor quibbles were also directed at the restricted visibility caused by the thick screen pillars and narrow windscreen, and the lack of fresh air vents in the cabin. But the Beetle's maintenance schedule (five grease points to attend to every 1,500 miles and an oil change every 3,000 miles) was still considered light by the standards of the day, and, surprisingly, 'superlatives are earned by the six-volt Hella headlamps, which give all the range and spread one could require'. The problem, as most Beetle owners found out, came once the electrical system had lost the first flush of youth and headlamps dimmed to obscurity.

Autocar's verdict was upbeat:

> Persistent mechanical development, as well as a progressive improvement in detail equipment and finish, have brought the VW to such a pitch of almost overall excellence that its reputation has never been higher. A hardy and economical beast of burden for the motoring masses, it is yet so individual in character and behaviour that many of the more sophisticated and experienced motorists cannot escape its charm.

1962 MODEL

The following year (August 1961 for the 1962 model year) saw a further batch of changes aimed at making the Beetle even more practical and easy to drive.

The traditional worm and nut type steering was replaced by a smoother and more accurate worm-and-roller system. Seat belt anchorage points (though not as yet the actual belts) were introduced for the first time, and vents were fitted in the heelboard panel below the rear seats to allow warm air into the rear of the car. These could be closed off if desired so that all the air was directed onto the windscreen.

The front bonnet now had self-supporting struts, the fuel tank was redesigned to give extra luggage space and a clever automatic windscreen washer was fitted. Simply pressurize the bottle using an air hose at a garage forecourt, and it would retain sufficient pressure to squirt the whole litre of washer fluid onto the windscreen at the touch of a button.

At long last a fuel gauge was fitted to the left of the speedometer, allowing the familiar reserve fuel tap in the footwell to be consigned to history. This modification came as a relief for many drivers, who had put up with the absence of such a basic instrument as a fuel gauge for far too long – more than four years previously, US magazine *Road & Track* had complained that 'there is still no factory-installed gas gauge or warning light, and the momentary panic of running out of gas and switching to the reserve in the midst of traffic is as unpleasant as ever'.

Typically, the fuel gauge was fitted only to the Export model, and not to the standard Beetle which by now looked quite outdated, a living fossil by comparison with the much-evolved Export model. The standard Beetle soldiered on with the 30bhp

One small step for motoring, but a major leap forward for the Beetle! In 1961, UK-spec Beetles were at long last fitted with a fuel gauge, and the emergency fuel reserve tap was consigned to history.

engine, crash gearbox and, amazingly, cable brakes. Its trim was spartan, with bumpers, hub caps and door handles being painted not chromed, but doubtless buyers forgave its shortcomings for the price saving it offered over the Export version.

1963 MODEL

The early to mid-1960s saw relatively few changes to the Beetle – probably because the VW factory had their hands full with the Type 3 that they had launched in 1961. Neglect meant that the Beetle started to fall behind the newer models that continually arrived on the scene. The latter half of the decade saw a flurry of Beetle development as VW strove – with spectacular success – to recapture the ground that had been lost.

One much-appreciated modification that was made late in 1962 (to appear on 1963

model year cars) was a revised heating system. Until now, heat had been provided by ducting into the cabin air that had been warmed by passing over the cylinders and heating elements attached to the exhaust pipes. Mostly this arrangement worked well enough, but as Ford had been eager to point out to its sales staff, it could under certain conditions lead to oil and exhaust fumes contaminating the incoming air, to the discomfort of the occupants.

The redesigned heating system employed a pair of heat exchangers mounted under each bank of engine cylinders. Fresh air was channelled through the heat exchangers, warmed, and ducted into the cabin without coming into actual contact with the engine.

Another of Ford's criticism's was answered by the adoption of a new easily cleaned vinyl headlining for the roof in place of the cloth original. Meanwhile, one of the Beetle's links with its past was

Several changes were made to the 1963 Beetle, but the casual observer wouldn't notice them. The heating system was improved, an easy-to-clean vinyl headlining was fitted in place of the cloth original, and the Wolfsburg crest on the bonnet was replaced by a VW logo.

severed when the Wolfsburg crest bonnet badge was replaced by the familiar VW emblem. The crest logo did, however, remain on the centre of the steering wheel.

Things stayed quiet in 1963, when changes were restricted to swapping the 'pope's nose' numberplate light pod for a wider, less shapely housing, fitting vinyl seat covers instead of cloth, and replacing the half-circle horn ring with a pair of buttons set into the steering-wheel spokes. A sliding steel sunroof was also added to the options list, replacing the roll-up cloth version.

1964 MODEL

A more significant modification came the following year, but it was so subtle that it was easy to miss – the front and rear screens were again slightly enlarged to improve visibility. And, in a first for the Beetle, the windscreen was now slightly curved.

As a consequence the windscreen wipers were lengthened, and now parked on the left-hand side of the screen base, not the right – which improved vision for drivers of right-hand-drive cars in wet weather.

A folding rear seat backrest was introduced, providing a useful increase in the amount of luggage space available inside the car, and the single heater knob on the chassis tunnel was replaced by two levers – the right-hand lever controlled all six heater vents, while the left-hand lever could be used to control just the two outlets in the rear. The T-shaped engine lid handle was also replaced by a more convenient lockable push-button item.

Minor changes like these were all very well, but the Beetle was starting to come in for increasing criticism in the face of competition from newer models. In particular, its lack of power and sometimes challenging handling attracted adverse comment. *Motor Trend* complained that 'the car's

For the 1965 model year, the Beetle was fitted with a slightly curved wind-screen for the first time. All glass panels increased in size and the A-posts were made thinner in an effort to improve visibility.

extremely susceptible to crosswinds – so much so that during really severe gusts you begin to feel like a ping-pong ball'.

Road Test noted that 'prospective pur-chasers are now taking a closer look at the opposition before automatically rushing out to buy a VW'. Their road tester grum-bled about having to take the Beetle back to the dealer every 1,500 miles (2,400km) for lubrication, and getting only a six-month warranty. And after pitting a Beetle against the new MG1100, their verdict was: 'Trade your VW for an MG1100? Go ahead.'

Volkswagen's answer to this sort of criti-cism was dramatic. A double whammy launch of new, more powerful Beetles – the 1300 in 1965 and the 1500 in 1966.

1300 BEETLE

The 1300 engine used the crank from the Type 3's 1.5-litre engine to lengthen its stroke from 64mm to 69mm, giving a total capacity of 1,285cc. Combined with an increase in compression ratio from 7.0:1 to 7.3:1, this resulted in a power output of 40bhp at 4,000rpm.

Despite the increase in power VW decid-ed to stick to the existing nine-inch drum brakes all round, but the front drums were strengthened, and ventilated wheels were adopted to increase the flow of cooling air over the brakes. Wheels on the 1300 were finished with a new set of flatter chromed hub caps.

Maintenance-free ball-joints replaced the king-pins on the front suspension, which meant that service intervals for the 1300 could be stretched to 6,000 miles (9,600km). The number of leaves in the front torsion bars received attention once again, increasing from eight to ten.

A '1300' chrome badge appeared on the engine lid, while inside an additional vent was added to the top of the dashboard to improve windscreen demisting, and the half-circle horn ring made a comeback in this model. The floor-mounted dipswitch

Beetle 1300 (1965–75)

Engine
Type	Air-cooled ohv flat-four, single-port cylinder heads (twin-port from 1970)
Capacity	1,285cc
Bore × stroke	77mm × 69mm
Compression ratio	7.3:1
Max. power	40bhp @ 4,000rpm
Max. torque	65lb/ft @ 2,000rpm

Transmission
Gearbox	Manual four-speed, synchro on all forward gears
Gear ratios	1st: 3.80
	2nd: 2.06
	3rd: 1.32
	4th: 0.89
	Reverse: 3.88
	Final drive: 4.38

Suspension
Front	Independent with transverse torsion bars and trailing arms; anti-roll bar
Rear	Independent with swing axles, transverse torsion bars and trailing arms; equalizer spring

Steering
Worm and roller

Brakes
Drum all-round

Dimensions (in/mm)
Length	160/4,070
Width	60/1,540
Weight	1,810lb (820kg)

Performance
0–60mph	23sec
30–50mph (top gear)	16sec
Top speed	76mph (122km/h)
Fuel consumption	32mpg (8.8l/100km)

With 40bhp on tap, the longer-stroke 1,285cc engine fitted to the 1300 Beetle provided a useful improvement in performance while still returning a competitive fuel consumption.

was incorporated into a column stalk, and new safety features included anti-burst door locks, stronger seat mountings and locking front seat backs.

Testing the new 1300, *Autocar* was lukewarm about the performance improvements:

> It is still built to be durable rather than lively and the output represents only 31bhp per litre . . . acceleration is therefore best described as adequate rather than brisk, and the 1300 takes 23sec to reach 60mph (100km/h) from a standstill. This is 4.5sec better than the previous model we tested (a 34bhp 1200) and all the other figures show similar gains.

Maximum speed has increased by 4mph to 75mph (120km/h) and one can now run up to higher speeds in the gears.

The engine came in for praise for starting immediately, warming up quickly, and displaying no flat-spots. The gearchange had softened up a bit since the early days, but was still reckoned to be better than average.

Autocar averaged 28.8mpg (9.8l/100km) in hard driving, and considered 30mpg (9.4l/100km) or more would be easily obtainable with a lighter right foot. Although one of the Beetle's attractions was its ability to cruise flat-out, dropping the cruising speed to 60mph brought a significant saving in fuel consumption of more than 10mpg. The engine, however, was famous for using no oil between changes.

The Beetle's handling still had its drawbacks, particularly in the wet when 'the tail can flick out in a trice and catch (the driver) unawares unless he studies the surfaces like a motorcyclist and expects oversteer at every turn'.

By now *Autocar* had changed its mind about the headlamps, which came in for scathing criticism. 'On dipped beam we could not see to drive faster than 50mph and the main beams were too narrow for road-wide illumination ahead'.

Beetle 1500 (1966–70)

Engine
Type	Air-cooled ohv flat-four, single-port cylinder heads
Capacity	1,493cc
Bore × stroke	83mm × 69mm
Compression ratio	7.5:1
Max. power	44bhp @ 4,000rpm
Max. torque	74lb ft @ 2,000rpm

Transmission
Gearbox	Manual four-speed, synchro on all forward gears
Gear ratios	1st: 3.80
	2nd: 2.06
	3rd: 1.26
	4th: 0.89
	Reverse: 3.61
	Final drive: 4.1

Suspension
Front	Independent with transverse torsion bars and trailing arms; anti-roll bar
Rear	Independent with swing axles, transverse torsion bars and trailing arms; equalizer spring

Steering
Worm and roller

Brakes
Front disc, rear drums

Dimensions (in/mm)
Length	160/4,060
Width	60/1,540
Weight	1,810lb (820kg)

Performance
0–60mph	18sec
30–50mph (top gear)	16sec
Top speed	78mph (125km/h)
Fuel consumption	30mpg (9.4l/100km)

Interestingly, *Autocar* also noted that Beetles had become such a common sight on British roads that the once common practice of owners waving at each other had died out. With annual production worldwide now exceeding one million units, they weren't about to get any rarer for a while yet. But *Autocar* did appreciate something of the Beetle's practical appeal, likening it to 'a pair of corduroy trousers; it is not stylish, it is not the height of comfort, yet it is terribly practical and durable and the kind of possession one can become attached to for no other reason than that it does its job effectively'.

1500 BEETLE

Charges of sluggish performance were countered almost straight away with the launch of the 1500 – or the 'Fifteen', as it was fondly nicknamed. This represented a massive step forward for the Beetle, with significantly more power, suspension revisions that went a long way to taming that wayward rear end, and, for the first time, front disc brakes.

An engine displacement of 1,493cc was obtained by boring out the cylinders of the 1300 unit from 77 to 83mm. At the same time the compression ratio was hiked to 7.5:1, to give an increased power output of 44bhp. More importantly, torque – the ability of a car to pull away at low revs – went up to 74lb ft at a relaxed 2,000rpm.

The 1500 and 1300 models were given a 1,350mm rear track (instead of the 1,250mm of the 1200). Their handling also benefited from a new equalizer spring that was attached to the rear suspension. This provided extra support to the rear torsion bars when they were loaded up, and significantly reduced the oversteer that could be experienced when the tyres reached the limit of their grip. Grip itself was still in relatively short supply thanks to the continued fitting of crossply tyres, but many owners soon switched to radials and consequently found their cars' roadholding vastly improved.

In accordance with American legislation, the engine lid was bent slightly to allow the rear number plate to be mounted vertically. Meanwhile, push-button door handles were fitted, and these could now be conveniently opened with the ignition key. Push-buttons allowed the doors to be locked from the inside.

Attention was paid to all switchgear to make it safer in the event of an accident, with the ash-tray knob being deleted and softer plastic used for other switches, now coloured black to cut out distracting reflections in the windscreen. The sides of the front seats were fitted with levers to make the task of tilting them easier.

To demonstrate the secure handling of the 1500, VW invited its UK dealers to launch parties at Silverstone and Oulton Park in September 1966, and told them to drive the cars round the circuits as hard as they liked. At this time, Beetle prices in the UK, including purchase tax, were: 1300 – £662; 1500 – £698; Cabriolet – £1,004. A sunroof for the saloons added an extra £48 to the total.

Autosport tested the 1500 and found it to be enjoyably nippy, and 'a safer car, with far better handling, feeling less tail-heavy than its predecessor'.

Autocar coaxed a top speed of 81mph (129.6km/h) from the 1500, and covered the 0-60mph (100km/h) sprint in 21.9 seconds. But the car's real strength lay in its effortless cruising abilities:

> The top gear mph per 1,000rpm figure of 19.5mph means that at the maximum speed of 81mph the engine is turning over

Thanks to a new rear suspension equalizer spring, the new 1500 was not only the quickest Beetle yet, but the best handling too. VW stressed the fact by launching the car at Silverstone race track.

at just below 4,200rpm. It takes only the slightest uphill gradient to slow the car, but with a tail wind or favourable slope, the accurate speedometer soon reaches the 90mph mark.

Less impressive, however, was the 'persistent clatter of the engine (which) is something that VW owners have to learn to live with'.

Fuel consumption, averaging 27.4mpg (10.3l/100km), was little worse than the 1300 tested previously.

VW's 'ingenious new design to reduce the inherent oversteer' was singled out for special praise:

> The result is to make the front wheels do a great deal more work on corners, thus giving the car an appreciable understeer initially. In the dry, the car can be cornered very fast indeed, with the tail just starting to break away when the limit is reached and the tyres are screaming in protest.

As ever, the Beetle displayed in its favour an outstanding finish and engineering quality, reliability and easy servicing. But *Autocar* could also produce a list of faults – the bottom-hinged pedals were awkward to use, the gear lever too far away, the hand-brake too near, the ventilation poor with no provision for cold air other than opening a window, and the heater output varied too much according to engine speed. *Autocar* concluded:

> As a VW Beetle the 1500 is undoubtedly the best VW Beetle yet, but the character of the car still takes one back at least a decade and despite the latest engine and other revisions several aspects of the VW show up to disadvantage against those of its competitor.

This was in late 1966, a year in which worldwide Beetle production remained comfortably above a million. Maybe the average Beetle buyer had different priorities to the average road tester. *Car Life*

appreciated this when they described the Beetle as 'still the best bargain in transportation short of a bicycle'. And hidden in a survey carried out by *Car South Africa* was a powerful reason to buy VW. Of the owners of 1966-67 1300s polled, over half had experienced no problems and would buy a Volkswagen again.

In the years immediately ahead the Beetle was to face its stiffest challenges yet. Safety considerations would further disfigure its good looks, and its rate of evolution would have to be stepped up to a frantic pace in order to maintain its competitiveness against new models. But in the loyalty and enthusiasm of its customers, the Beetle had a backbone of support that would see it thriving long after the motoring pundits had pronounced it dead many times over.

8 Adapt and Survive: the Super Beetles

In the late 1960s American legislators became increasingly preoccupied with car safety. This was laudable enough, but it led to a rash of sometimes ill-considered regulations being applied to areas of car specification that had previously been left to the discretion of engineers and designers.

This posed little problem for a manufacturer building a new car: the necessary concessions to US safety legislation were simply incorporated at the design stage. But for an existing model like the Beetle, it meant altering elements that had originally been designed to harmonize with the vehicle as the whole. Although the changes were often only minor ones, they had a disproportionate affect on the overall appearance of the Beetle.

The first batch of these changes initially appeared on American-spec Beetles, before being standardized on European models in August 1967 to feature on 1968 model year cars. The most striking change was the repositioning of the lights and bumpers. Out went the sloping headlamps, which blended smoothly into the curve of the front wings, and out went the elegant curved bumpers moulded round the lower extremities of the front and rear bodywork. In their place came upright headlamps slightly recessed into the wings, and chunkier bumpers mounted higher up the body.

Because of the raised bumper height, both the engine lid and bonnet had to be shortened. The valences were made correspondingly longer and the horn grilles deleted. At the rear, the lights were enlarged, and integral reversing lamps became an optional extra. Safety door handles, with an opening trigger concealed behind the handle, were also fitted.

Although this meant that the Beetle's good looks suffered this year, there were a series of other real improvements for Beetle owners to welcome. At long last came a switch from the Beetle's marginal six-volt electrical system to the twelve-volt electrics used by every other car. The 1200, however, soldiered on with six volts for another eight years.

Dual-circuit brakes – safer in the event of brake failure affecting part of the braking system – replaced the old single-circuit set-up (except, of course, on the perennially overlooked 1200) and the brake fluid reservoir moved to the inside of the left-hand inner front wing.

The fuel filler cap was also repositioned, so at long last there was no need to open the front bonnet to fill up with petrol. However, the new filler, mounted under a flap in the front wing, was not lockable and so was vulnerable to a thief with a siphon hose.

Another big improvement was that fresh cool air could now be fed into the cabin. Sucked in through louvres in the bonnet just in front of the windscreen, the air is channelled through a pair of hoses and out

From the 1968 model year onwards Beetles looked very different. Upright headlamps replaced the sloping originals, bumpers were repositioned higher up the bodywork and the engine lid and bonnet were shortened.

Adopting twelve-volt electrics in 1967 was – literally speaking – a bright move for the Beetle, banishing the six-volt model's anaemic lighting and tardy cold-weather starting (the 1200 model stuck to the six-volt system for another eight years, though).

After 1967 the Beetle's dashboard looked barer than ever, with the fuel gauge incorporated into the speedometer, but the repositioning of the ignition switch on the steering column was a welcome improvement.

of two extra vents cut in the top of the dashboard. These vents are opened or closed by turning knobs fitted to the facia below the radio.

The facia itself was simplified by incorporating the fuel gauge within the speedometer dial, and a black, padded, dashboard was made available as an option. Another useful change was the repositioning of the ignition switch from its awkward site on the passenger's half of the dashboard (in right-hand-drive cars) to the right of the steering column – safe now from errant children in the passenger seat playing their favourite trick of turning off the ignition while daddy is driving.

BEETLE AUTOMATIC

The biggest departure from traditional VW practice came with the introduction of a Beetle Automatic. The three-speed automatic option was first made available with the 1500 model, with the 1300 following suit in 1968, and the 1600 in 1970. In fact it wasn't a true automatic at all, but a semi-automatic, which had a conventional

gear shift but no clutch pedal.

As a by-product of its new transmission, the semi-automatic Beetle gained much-improved handling characteristics. This came about because the torque converter that came with the automatic gearbox was about an inch longer than the clutch housing of the manual car. It encroached on the rear suspension, which had to be redesigned to make room. The swing-axles were made double-jointed, in a similar fashion to the layout used by Porsche's rear-engined 911. This countered their tendency to jack up and lose traction under extreme cornering. It was a paradox that the semi-automatic Beetle – destined mostly for American drivers who didn't like the hassle of changing gears – was given a suspension better suited to more testing European conditions.

Autocar, sampling a 1500 Automatic, found that in the dry at least the modified rear suspension dramatically reduced the Beetle's tail-happiness:

The car starts off as an understeerer, and remains that way at normal, touring cornering speeds. In fact, if you go into a

Beetle 1500 Auto (1967–70)

Engine

Type	Air-cooled ohv flat-four, single-port cylinder heads
Capacity	1,493cc
Bore × stroke	83mm × 69mm
Compression ratio	7.5:1
Max. power	44bhp @ 4,000rpm
Max. torque	74lb/ft @ 2,000rpm

Transmission

Gearbox	Semi-automatic three-speed, torque-converter and electro-pneumatic clutch
Gear ratios	1st: 2.06
	2nd: 1.26
	3rd: 0.89
	Reverse: 3.07
	Final drive: 4.38

Suspension

Front	Independent with transverse torsion bars and trailing arms; anti-roll bar
Rear	Independent with double-jointed drive shafts, semi-trailing arms and transverse torsion bars

Steering

Worm and roller

Brakes

Front disc, rear drums

Dimensions (in/mm)

Length	160/4,060
Width	61/1,540
Weight	1,808lb (820kg)

Performance

0–60mph	23sec
30–50mph (top gear)	17sec
Top speed	74mph (118km/h)
Fuel consumption	28mpg (10.1l/100km)

corner too fast you can scrub off the excess speed by turning more acutely into the corner. In extreme conditions the inside front wheel lifts (which the driver feels as a lurch) and the car stays on its rightful side of the road without swinging wide. If you lift off suddenly in a corner there is very little change in the feel of the car, and it continues safely on course. On a wet road, though, it often feels as though the tail might get the upper hand, and greasy corners need a lot of respect.

US magazine *Foreign Car Guide* loved the semi-auto, declaring it to be worth the extra cost over the manual for the modified

Almost an automatic

Americans loved their Bugs and by 1967 they were buying 300,000 of them each year. What a lot of Americans weren't so keen on was having to change their Beetle's gears manually – automatics have always been vastly more popular in the US than in Europe. But the Beetle was available only in manual form.

So, reckoned VW, one way to give the Beetle extra appeal, particularly in the all-important US market, was to fit it with an automatic transmission. In 1967 they duly launched the 1500 Automatic (soon afterwards followed by a 1300 auto, and, in 1971, by a 1600 auto).

Except that the Beetle Automatic wasn't a true automatic. It dispensed with the clutch pedal, but retained the manual gear lever, so that shifting from cog to cog was still the driver's responsibility.

Like a true automatic, the Beetle's semi-automatic system features a torque converter, so that the car creeps forward if left in gear at traffic lights, and holds itself on a slope. The three-speed gearbox is simply the standard Beetle 'box with first gear removed. The remaining gears are arranged in an H-pattern with reverse where first used to be. The bottom ratio is where you find second in a manual 'box, but is renamed 'low range'. The next two slots – 'Drive 1' and 'Drive 2' - thus represent the third and fourth gears of a manual car.

To change gear, you simply move the lever from one slot to the next. Microswitches at the base of the lever activate a servo-operated clutch, disengaging it when the lever is moved out of gear and re-engaging it when the lever reaches the slot for the next gear.

The switches that operate the clutch are quite sensitive, so if you like to drive around with your hand resting on the gearstick, a semi-auto will soon cure you of the habit. Long-legged drivers may also find that they inadvertently knock the car out of gear with their left knee. The throttle must be used sensitively if smooth shifts are to be made. It's necessary to lift off while changing up, and on downshifts a blip on the throttle before letting go of the gearstick helps make the change smooth.

Low range was recommended for moving off uphill, or with a heavy load. In normal driving most drivers would leave the gear stick in Drive 1. Thanks to the torque converter, the car could be driven in this ratio from a standstill up to 70mph (110km/h). Of course, Drive 2 – the equivalent of the manual car's top gear – would be best for fast cruising. So effective was the torque converter that the car could actually be left in Drive 2 all the time, although acceleration became snail-like, and the fluid in the torque converter was in danger of overheating if it was forced to do too much work (if the torque converter does start to overheat, a warning light flashes to tell you to change down a gear).

Neither a true manual or a true auto, the semi-auto arrangement offers either the best or the worst of both worlds, depending on your point of view. It does give the driver more control than a standard automatic transmission. Against this, as *Autocar* reported, the semi-auto was over five seconds slower than the manual from 0–60mph, and 2mpg thirstier as well. With the 1500 Auto costing £861 4s 10d at launch, £83 more than the manual version, the semi-auto 'box was a pricey option too.

US magazine *World Car Guide* wondered whether the semi-auto option was worth the extra money. 'We are inclined to say no. The semi-automatic doesn't add all that much to the simplicity of Beetle driving. Indeed, some might say that it detracts from the simplicity'.

The one thing most people did like about the semi-automatic was its double-jointed rear suspension. This modification had to be made to create room for the torque converter, and as a welcome side-effect it made the handling of this particular model much more secure.

Although the semi-auto did enjoy some success, particularly in the US where by 1970 it accounted for almost one in every five Beetles sold, it was generally regarded as an oddity and its devotees, though often enthusiastic, remained comparatively few in number. A true automatic Beetle would certainly have been a better seller, but that was an option which the world was never offered.

rear suspension alone.

After such major upheavals, Volkswagen took things a little easier for a couple of years to follow, though there were, of course, the usual procession of minor modifications. The petrol filler flap was now not openable from outside the car, which deterred the petrol pinchers. It was released instead by pulling a handle situated under the dashboard by the driver's right foot.

The release handle for the bonnet was also moved, from down in the passenger footwell to a more convenient location inside the glovebox. The heating vents on the sills were moved back below the doors, and were controlled by separate levers. The Beetle also gained the safety feature of hazard warning lights.

In the August of 1968, the semi-automatic option was extended to the 1300 as well as the 1500 and, happily for buyers in the US, the superior rear suspension of the semi-auto was made standard there on manual versions. The 1300 also now offered the option of front disc brakes. Prices in the UK in 1968 were £670 for the 1200, £750 for the 1300 and £795 for the 1500.

In 1969 an optional luxury package was offered for the 1300 and 1500, and cars fitted with it displayed an L on their engine lid badge. This package included a padded black dashboard, anti-dazzle rear-view mirror, a lockable glovebox lid, plusher carpets, bumpers with black rubber inserts and reversing lights built into the rear light clusters.

Both the 1500 and the Cabriolet gained louvres in their engine lids for better cooling. This especially benefited the Cabrio, which had always suffered from marginal engine cooling. Because of its folding hood, it lacked the vents which saloons had in the bodywork below their rear screens.

Inside, the hot air vents in the sills gained simple sliding covers to turn them on and off, and the wheels were now painted silver, instead of the rather more elegant traditional black and cream.

Advances in engine technology meant that the Beetle was now starting to lose its claim to be a cheap car to run. Testing a 1300 against five main rivals, *Motor* found the Beetle to be slowest in acceleration and outright speed – and easily the most thirsty of the pack too.

But the Beetle still enjoyed wholehearted support from its owners. Beetle buyers found their cars to be reliable and built to last and, when it was time for them to change cars, most unhesitatingly returned for a second helping. Comparisons with other manufacturers of similarly priced cars showed VW in a glowing light. This, remember, was at a time when the quality standard of British cars was falling through the floor, with cars such as the notoriously unreliable Austin Maxi, launched in 1969, helping to turn the British car industry into a national joke.

Car, a magazine not noted for pulling its punches, pondered the question of why the Beetle, such an obviously outdated design, still managed to take three per cent of the UK market. The answer was quality. *Car* contrasted the Beetle to the Rootes Avenger, with which it was 'a fight even to get the tinny key in the rusty, mean little lock in the flexible door panel. With the VW, the key itself felt properly made'.

The Beetle's door handle had a 'crisp, trigger-action', its lock gave a 'solid thunk', and the door opened and closed like a Rolls-Royce's. Quality shone through in other areas too, said *Car*: 'VWs were noisy beasts at one time, but VW's engineers know all about insulation these days'. Unlike the disappointing products passed off as cars by British Leyland, the report concluded, with a Beetle 'you really feel you're getting

Super Beetle 1302 (1970–2)

Engine
Type	Air-cooled ohv flat-four, twin-port cylinder heads
Capacity	1,285cc
Bore × stroke	77mm × 69mm
Compression ratio	7.5:1
Max. power	44bhp @ 4,100rpm
Max. torque	65lb/ft @ 3,000rpm

Transmission
Gearbox	Manual four-speed, synchro on all forward gears
Gear ratios	1st: 3.80
	2nd: 2.06
	3rd: 1.26
	4th: 0.88
	Reverse: 3.61
	Final drive: 4.38

Suspension
Front	Independent with MacPherson struts; anti-roll bar
Rear	Independent with double-jointed drive shafts, semi-trailing arms and transverse torsion bars

Steering
Worm and roller

Brakes
Drum all-round

Dimensions (in/mm)
Length	1611/4,080mm
Width	2062/1,585mm
Weight	1,950lb (870kg)

Performance
0–60mph	21sec
30–50mph (top gear)	15sec
Top speed	78mph (125km/h)
Fuel consumption	27mpg (10.5l/100km)

your money's worth of honest motor engineering'.

Motor, carrying out a survey of owners of 1300 and 1500 Beetles, discovered that respondents' cars had been nearly 100 per cent reliable. Only half as many faults were reported as for the previous best performer – the Cortina 1600 – and 66 per cent of owners said they'd buy a Beetle again.

Strong though its customer support was, Volkswagen knew that unless continuing improvements were made to keep the Beetle competitive with newer models this loyalty could evaporate overnight. So, in 1970 there came another major package of changes which distanced the Beetle still

Super Beetle 1302S (1970–2)

Engine

Type	Air-cooled ohv flat-four, twin-port cylinder heads
Capacity	1,584cc
Bore × stroke	85.5mm × 69mm
Compression ratio	7.5:1
Max. power	50bhp @ 4,000rpm
Max. torque	79lb ft @ 2,800rpm

Transmission

Gearbox	Manual four-speed, synchro on all forward gears
Gear ratios	1st: 3.80
	2nd: 2.06
	3rd: 1.26
	4th: 0.88
	Reverse: 3.61
	Final drive: 4.1

Suspension

Front	Independent with MacPherson struts; anti-roll bar
Rear	Independent with double-jointed drive shafts, semi-trailing arms and transverse torsion bars

Steering — Worm and roller

Brakes — Front discs, rear drums

Dimensions (in/mm)

Length	160/4,080
Width	62/1,585
Weight	1,920lb (870kg)

Performance

0–60mph	18sec
30–50mph (top gear)	15sec
Top speed	80mph (125km/h)
Fuel consumption	25mpg (11.3l/100km)

further from the car created by Ferdinand Porsche thirty-five years earlier.

SUPER BEETLE

Most dramatic was the introduction of a brand new Beetle model – the Super Beetle. Two versions were available: the 1302 with a 44bhp 1,285cc engine, and the 50bhp 1,584cc 1302S.

The Super Beetles looked quite distinctive from the older Beetle models – and the differences went more than skin deep. Both

With its uncomfortably bulging front bonnet line, the 1302 was hardly the prettiest Beetle ever. However, buyers appreciated its extra luggage space and more powerful engine, and it gave sales a new lease of life.

Because the MacPherson strut front suspension took up less room than the torsion bar system, the Super models boasted an impressive increase in front boot space, with the spare wheel now stowing flat.

1300 and 1600 engines were given new twin inlet port cylinder heads which improved engine breathing. This pushed the power output of the 1300 up from 40 to 44bhp. The 1600 was essentially a 1500 unit, bored out to compensate for the power-sapping emissions equipment that had to be fitted in the US.

The good news on the suspension front was that the 1302 models received the double-jointed axles from the semi-automatic, and their handling benefited accordingly. Meanwhile, at the front end the suspension was given a dramatic overhaul, with torsion bars being replaced by MacPherson struts. The main benefit of the MacPherson strut arrangement was that they took up much less space than torsion bars, and allowed the amount of luggage space under the front bonnet to be greatly enlarged. The position of the spare wheel was changed, and it now sat neatly flat in front of the petrol tank, which itself was moved backwards. Front disc brakes were fitted as standard on the 1302S, and were optional on the 1302.

There was one drawback to the new front suspension. Because the front wings, valance and bonnet all needed reshaping to accommodate the tall MacPherson strut assemblies, the Beetle's looks suffered once again. Its front end now looked uncomfortably bloated, like an ageing boxer's bulging nose.

Ventilation was, however, improved on the Super Beetle with the addition of a fresh air through-flow system, including crescent-shaped vents fitted behind both rear windows.

The existing 1200 and 1300 models continued to sell alongside the Super Beetles, although the 1500 was now dropped. The 1970 Beetle range, therefore, comprised the 34bhp torsion bar 1200, the 44bhp torsion bar 1300 (which had also gained the new twin-port engine), the 44bhp MacPherson strut 1302 and the 50bhp MacPherson strut 1302S. At £875, the 1302S cost £63 more than the 1500 it replaced.

Autocar, testing a 1302S, commented that even though the 1600 engine boasted a power increase of 14 per cent over the old 1500, its total output of 50bhp was still:

> very modest for the size of engine. There can hardly be another engine left in production which turns out only 31bhp per litre. However, aided by what is a smooth and low-drag body shape, even 50bhp is enough to give the Beetle a top speed of 80mph (125km/h). Even at the maximum, engine revs are only 4,050rpm so this speed can be held for cruising all day long.

With a 0–60mph sprint of 18.3sec, the 1302S beat the 1500 that *Autocar* had previously tested by some 3.5sec, and it reached its top speed downwind from rest in just 45sec. Fuel consumption, however, had taken a turn for the worse. Overall, the 1302S returned just 24mpg (11.8l/100km), compared with the old 1500's 27mpg (10.5l/100km).

The extra luggage space under the bonnet impressed the tester, who remarked that it 'is quite amazing what can be packed in and not foul the lid when it shuts down'.

On the handling front, the MacPherson struts made little difference: 'As far as the driver notices, the front end behaves much the same as before, although there does seem to be a little more bump-thump and road noise on some surfaces. Steering effort is heavier than before.' The double-jointed rear suspension did a good job of tying down the rear end, though. 'At the limit on a wet road it is the front end which lets go first and it is only by deliberate and clumsy misuse of the brakes that the tail can be made to flick out of line.'

However, 'in spite of the considerable suspension improvements, the Beetle still gets badly blown about by side gusts. Battling up the M1 motorway at 70mph (110km/h) called for quite a lot of courage and often more road than the width of one lane.'

Despite the improvements to the car's ventilation arrangement, this still came in for criticism:

The new fresh air system has been skimped to get it in behind the existing facia and it passes only a gentle warm breeze, never a real cooling blast. Whereas two levers and a switch do all that is required on most other cars, the VW system is operated by a total of eight controls, scattered all round the car.

Despite all the engineering improvements, a lot of faults in the Beetle still go on. Things like the new ventilation system are a step in the right direction and the extra acceleration and better cornering are worth having. Like the 1500 Beetle before it, it is the best Beetle yet, but it still comes a long way behind its competitors in qualities like styling, comfort and prestige. Even at the latest price of £875, though, it represents good value for money especially if one takes into account the all-important resale value and long-term running costs.

Road & Track (*R&T*) largely concurred with *Autocar*'s verdict, calling the 1600 Super Beetle 'the best Beetle yet, but still not as good as the competition'. *R&T* praised the car's 'exceptionally good' fuel economy – compared, of course, with the average American gas guzzler – but attacked its noise under acceleration, sticky gear change, sensitivity to sidewinds

at high speed, bouncy ride, brakes (drums all round for the American market) and ventilation. It concluded:

The Beetle, whether in standard or Super form, has three main points to recommend it: fuel economy, workmanship and its reputation for long life and good service. If you value those three virtues above all others, then the Beetle is for you. Otherwise it is hopelessly outdated and outdone by both Japanese and American economy cars.

The car-buying public appeared to take a different view. In 1971, boosted by the introduction of the Super Beetle, worldwide production reached an all-time high of 1,219,612, and in that same year, US buyers snapped up more than 330,000 Beetles.

As was usual after a year of upheaval, VW confined the next year's changes to minor details. The most obvious difference inside a 1972 model year car is the steering wheel, a four-spoke item which has a flat soft plastic centre to reduce the likelihood of chest injuries in a crash. The windscreen wipe/wash switch moved from a button on the dashboard to a stalk on the right of the steering column.

In yet another effort to improve ventilation, an extra vent was added to the two existing openings on the pillar next to the rear screen. The rear screen itself was made taller, increasing the screen area by eleven per cent. Additional cooling louvres appeared on the engine lid to resemble those already on the cabriolet. VW also added to the Beetle's elderly engine the surprisingly advanced feature of electronic diagnosis. It could be plugged into a dealer's service computer to carry out 88 checks on the engine's state of health.

For the UK, VW brightened up the Beetle by offering a range of new colours –

pastel white, turquoise metallic, gentian blue, silver metallic, brilliant orange, Sumatra green, gemini metallic, kasan red, Texas yellow and marina blue. They publicized the fact by releasing a promotional Beetle painted in lurid stripes like a psychedelic zebra. This was nicknamed the 'Ballyhoo Beetle', though few enlivened the roads as, disappointingly, only a few were made and they were never sold as an official special edition.

In August 1972 came the latest and last major change to the Beetle's styling. The Super Beetles were rebadged as 1303 and 1303S, fitted with the twin-port 1,300 and 1,600cc engines respectively. They carried over the MacPherson strut front end from the 1302 models, but added a larger windscreen. This so-called panoramic screen, which had a much more pronounced curvature than before, was actually a remarkable forty-two per cent bigger. It did wonders for forward vision but looked uncomfortably out of proportion with the rest of the Beetle.

Like so many recent Beetle developments, the 1303 had been designed to meet new safety proposals in the US, and it cost VW millions to make the necessary changes. The top edge of the bonnet had to be shortened to make room for the new windscreen, and at the same time the bonnet lost its VW badge. The rear wheel arches were widened to accommodate much bigger rear light clusters.

The changes continued inside, with a completely new dashboard appearing. Moulded from black plastic, this was safer and more up-to-date than the Beetle's traditional metal dashboard. The speedometer sat in a shroud which cut down reflections and made it easier to read, while swivelling air vents were fitted at both ends of the dashboard, in a final stab at improving the Beetle's oft-criticized ventilation.

The seat mountings were strengthened, and now allowed greater for-and-aft adjustability. Because of this, both the gear lever and handbrake were moved backwards.

Australian magazine *Modern Motor* was enthusiastic about the new windscreen, saying 'this simple effective change has transformed the interior of the VW Superbug from a claustrophobic suitcase to an open spacious small sedan'. They also loved the 'real' dashboard, and the huge rear lights which 'could double as billy-cans, soup plates, crash helmets or hatboxes'.

Although annual production for 1973 was still at the astonishingly high figure of 1,206,018, it was clear that the curtain was starting to close on the Beetle. In the light of soaring petrol prices and the introduction of a new generation of efficient front-wheel-drive family hatchbacks – not least of all Volkswagen's own Polo and Golf – the next year's production was set to nose-dive to 791,000, and then to below half a million in 1975. Demand for the Beetle from its loyal and enthusiastic followers would continue for some years, but Volkswagen had now set its sights elsewhere, and had other priorities than developing the Beetle much further.

In 1973 the Super Beetles received self-stabilizing steering geometry, designed to counter the tendency of the car to wander under braking and reduce the chance of losing control in the event of a blow-out. An alternator replaced the engine dynamo on the Super Beetles. A luxury package became available for them, and cars fitted with it were badged 1303L and 1303LS.

The following year, the Super Beetles had their worm and roller steering (fitted since 1961, when it had replaced the original worm and nut system) replaced by a more direct and accurate rack and pinion set-up. Meanwhile the front indicators were repositioned from the wings into the bumper, and – for some obscure reason – the rear number plate light pod was treated to a row of corrugations.

US cars – which were by now distinguished from European models by hefty 5mph (8km/h)-impact bumpers – received fuel injection and catalytic converters in an effort to clean up their engines to meet increasingly stringent exhaust emissions regulations.

Meanwhile, there remained the 1200, cheap, utilitarian and as spartan as ever. After all these years, it still featured torsion bars all-round, with rear swing-axles

---

Super Beetle 1303 (1972–5)

Engine

Type	Air-cooled ohv flat-four, twin-port cylinder heads
Capacity	1,285cc
Bore × stroke	77mm × 69mm
Compression ratio	7.5:1
Max. power	44bhp @ 4,100rpm
Max. torque	65lb/ft @ 3,000rpm

Transmission

Gearbox	Manual four-speed, synchro on all forward gears
Gear ratios	1st: 3.78
	2nd: 2.06
	3rd: 1.26
	4th: 0.93
	Reverse: 3.79
	Final drive: 4.38

Suspension

Front	Independent with Macpherson struts; anti-roll bar
Rear	Independent with double-jointed drive shafts, semi-trailing arms and transverse torsion bars

Steering

Worm and roller (rack and pinion from 1974)

Brakes

Drum all-round

Dimensions (in/mm)

Length	162/4,110
Width	62/1,585
Weight	1,960lb (890kg)

Performance

0–60mph	21sec
30–50mph (top gear)	17sec
Top speed	78mph (125km/h)
Fuel consumption	26mpg (10.9l/100km)

A larger panoramic windscreen distinguished the 1303. It certainly improved visibility, and gave the Beetle a lighter and more airy feel inside, but again it did nothing for the car's looks.

Super Beetle 1303S (1972–5)

Engine
Type	Air-cooled ohv flat-four, twin-port cylinder heads, two overhead valves per cylinder
Capacity	1584cc
Bore × stroke	86mm × 69mm
Compression ratio	7.5:1
Max. power	50bhp @ 4,000rpm
Max. torque	79lb/ft @ 2,800rpm

Transmission
Gearbox	Manual four-speed, synchro on all forward gears
Gear ratios	1st: 3.78
	2nd: 2.06
	3rd: 1.26
	4th: 0.93
	Reverse: 3.79
	Final drive: 3.88

Suspension

Front	Independent with MacPherson struts; anti-roll bar
Rear	Independent with double-jointed drive shafts, semi-trailing arms and transverse torsion bars

Steering   Worm and roller (rack and pinion from 1974)

Brakes   Front discs, rear drums

Dimensions (in/mm)

Length	162/4,110
Width	62/1,585
Weight	1,960lb (890kg)

Performance

0–60mph	18sec
30–50mph (top gear)	15sec
Top speed	80mph (128km/h)
Fuel consumption	24mpg (11.8l/100km)

A black plastic safety dashboard arrived with the 1303. The speedometer was housed in a shroud to cut down reflections, and swivelling fresh-air vents were installed at both ends of the dashboard.

and worm and roller steering. It had painted bumpers and no passenger sun visor, ran on six-volt electrics and still had a reserve fuel tank instead of a fuel gauge. In 1974 the 1200 became even more down-to-earth, with black painted exhaust tail pipes and plastic hub caps instead of chrome plated ones – even the glovebox lid was deleted.

Production of the Super Beetles ceased in 1975, although the 1600 twin-port engine was still available, in a torsion-bar body and with front disc brakes. This model was, confusingly, badged the 1200S. The 1300 twin-port engine was also delet-

ed. The basic 1200, meanwhile, at long last received the benefits of twelve-volt electrics. It was one of these 1200s that was the last Beetle ever to roll off the German production lines, at VW's Emden factory in January 1978.

The Super Beetle lived on for a few years yet, however, in the shape of the Cabriolet, which was based on the 1303 until the very end. Safety scares had hit convertible models hard in the US during the mid-1970s, and this looked like killing off the Beetle Cabriolet there. But an unexpected resurgence of American interest in the Cabriolet gave it an extra lease of life. A Beetle

Special edition Beetles

There's a sure way to tell when a model is getting near the end of its life – count the special editions. As a model starts to fall behind newer competitors, it's a favourite ploy for manufacturers to dress a version up with special trim and an attractive specification, give it a special name, and hope it will tempt back straying purchasers.

The Beetle was no exception. When it became obvious that the Beetle had reached the point where little more development was possible, VW came up with a number of snappily dressed special editions, particularly aimed at younger, more fashion-conscious, buyers.

These special editions varied so much from market to market that it's impossible to do more than take a brief look at some of the more popular ones. Some of the special editions were hardly worth the effort, while others were very appealing variations on the Beetle theme.

One particularly desirable special edition was the GT. This was exclusive to Britain, and it was launched in 1972 in a limited run of 2,500 to celebrate the import of the 300,000th British Beetle. It featured the 50bhp 1600 engine in the 1300 torsion bar body – a combination that gave it a nifty turn of acceleration allied to sporty, entertaining handling.

Outside, the GT was distinguished by a vivid red, green or yellow paint-scheme, a GT engine lid badge, sports wheels and the large rear lights from the 1303. Inside, there was a padded black dashboard, wooden gear knob, and cloth-covered seats on 1303-style safety mountings. Today, the GT is a sought-after model.

The year of the GT, 1972, was also the year that the Beetle beat the production record of 15,007,033 set by the Model T Ford back in 1927. VW released a special edition, *Der Weltmeister* (The World Champion) to celebrate. As the record-breaking Beetle had been a 1302S, the German version of the World Champion Beetle was based, logically enough, on that model. In the UK, VW must have been keener to shift the standard 1300, because it was that version that our World Champion Beetle was based on.

The 1,500 UK World Champions were finished in Marathon metallic blue, which led them to become popularly known as the Marathon Beetles. Ten-spoke Lemmerz steel wheels were fitted. Buyers received a commemorative medal to stick on the dashboard and a World Champion booklet which recounted the Beetle's history.

The following year, 1973, was a bumper one for Beetle special editions. The Jeans Beetle was a

Jeans Bug was one of many special editions released to perk up Beetle sales in the 1970s.

cheap and cheerful special based on the 1200. With yellow paintwork, 'jeans' motifs, matching black headlamp rims, door handles, bumpers and engine lid handle, sports wheels and blue denim seats, the Jeans special edition was a striking car and one that appealed strongly to younger Beetle fans. Some 50,000 were made between late 1973 and the end of 1975, though their exact specifications varied between countries.

Several special editions were based on the Super Beetle. The City Beetle was a 1303 with sports wheels, a padded steering wheel, heated rear window, reversing lights, plush carpets and inertia-reel seatbelts. The Big Beetle, based on the 1303S, had all this plus wider wheels – 5.5J versus the City Beetle's 4.5J items.

An even sportier version was the Yellow and Black Racer, with low-profile tyres on 5.5J sports wheels, sports seats, a leather-trimmed steering wheel and – you guessed it – yellow and black paintwork (the engine lid and bonnet being finished in matt black). A total of 3,500 were made.

Special editions didn't die with the last of the European Beetles – Volkswagen de Mexico took them up with great enthusiasm. Their special editions have included the Silver Bug in 1981, which marked the 20-millionth Beetle produced, and, 11 years and another million Beetles later, the '21 Millones'. There have also been a Mexican Jeans Bug (1982), Aubergine Bug (1983), Velvet Red Bug (1984) and Winter and Sunny Bugs (1984).

In 1985 came a particularly 'special' Special, the Jubilee, which marked the Beetle's official 50th anniversary, and formed the last consignment of Beetles that VW ever officially exported from Mexico to Europe. The Jubilee featured elegant Pewter Grey paintwork, a Golf GTi-style steering wheel, sports wheels, tinted glass, and came with '50 Jähre Käfer' badges which owners could fix to the engine lid and front three-quarter panels.

Such was the interest in these epoch-marking cars that they sold out before they had even arrived in Europe. Unfortunately, fate failed to smile on these particularly attractive Beetles – severe weather caused almost the whole batch to be damaged while in transit to Europe, and they had to be rushed to VW's Hanover factory to receive emergency repairs before being despatched to their buyers.

Der letzte Käfer.

The last Beetle. The Jubilee special edition of 1985 marked both the Beetle's official fiftieth birthday, and Volkswagen's decision to end European imports of Beetles from Mexico, where the Jubilee was built.

Cabriolet suddenly became *the* car to be seen in, and sales of Cabriolets in America, having dipped to below 4,000 per year in the mid-1970s, made a startling recovery and exceeded 10,000 in 1979.

US magazine *Motor Trend* marvelled that the Beetle:

> has rejected its humble origins, forgotten its simple forebears and become, yes, the darling of the DiscoSuedes.

USC cheerleaders in tassled Nikes troop in from Beverley Hills to buy white-on-white convertibles. Westchester matrons in Amalfis order them black-on-black. In Fort Worth, orange is big, a nice Southwestern contrast to $100 layered jeans. In Fairfield County, the Saks and Bonwit shoppers are not particular about colour; the VW convertible is simply another outer garment to go with the current multi-skin look favoured by suburban matrons. For at $7,000, out the door, the once diffident bug has taken on a new aristocratic mien; it is the status car of the rank-conscious; the new-wave image of the born-again profligate; the adorable ornament of the Highway Culture.

But even this enthusiasm for the Cabriolet

wasn't enough to keep it in production indefinitely. In January 1980 the last example left Karmann's Osnabrück factory, and European production had finally ended.

But although Beetle production might have ceased in Europe, in other parts of the world, most notably Mexico and Brazil, it was still going strong. As long as the Beetle's unique combination of toughness, reliability, simplicity and cheapness lasted, it would still be in demand somewhere.

VW continued to make Mexican Beetles available in Europe by special order until 1985. Even when these imports came to an end, a few European enthusiasts, refusing to be denied their fix of brand-new Beetle, resorted to importing them on their own behalf. The trickle of new Beetles onto the roads of Europe continues to this day.

Aussie magazine Modern Motor *loved the 1303's huge rear light clusters, which 'could double as billy-cans, soup plates, crash helmets or hatboxes'.*

Karmann's Cabriolet (this is a 1974 model) continued to be based on the 1303 till production ceased in 1980. In its later years the Cabrio became highly fashionable in the US.

159

9 People's Beetles

Ferdinand Porsche had big ambitions for the Volkswagen that he sat down to design in the 1930s. He wanted it to become cheap transport for the masses, a car for the ordinary working person who previously had to make do with a bicycle.

This was a task the Beetle was admirably suited for, and despite the interruption of war, it ultimately succeeded in bringing cheap transportation to millions of people all over the world. In countries like Mexico and Brazil, it still serves this function today. But Ferdinand Porsche would have been staggered if he had known just how great an impact, above and beyond this basic function, his Beetle was to make on 20th century life.

Fantastic though it might have sounded to Porsche, his utilitarian little motor car became the most popular foreign car in America, selling in total more than 4.5 million in that land of luxury and materialism. And far from appealing simply on the merits of practicality and low cost, it attracted an extraordinary range of buyers, from Greenwich Village intellectuals to Hollywood starlets. Peter Sellers, John Lennon and Sean Connery all at one time joined the ranks of Beetle owners. The Beetle has even been used as a getaway car by LA gangsters.

Stranger still, this down-to-earth car, with its basic, low-power engine, inspired hordes of enthusiasts to tune and tweak it till it performed like a blood-and-guts sports car. Many fell so in love with its simple body styling that they would spend months lowering, modifying and repainting their car till it represented their peak of automotive perfection.

Others have done even weirder things with the Beetle. Malc Buchanan fitted a propeller to his and crossed the Irish Sea in it, taking seven hours for the 35-mile voyage. This pastime became so popular that followers formed a club, Waterbugs of America. Others have delighted in cramming record-breaking numbers of people inside a Beetle – one mountaineering club managed a mind-boggling fifty-seven. There have been innumerable models, statues and paintings of the Beetle, and it's had a host of accessories, from T-shirts to toilet-roll holders, fashioned in its image.

The Beetle even became a film star. Herbie, star of *The Love Bug*, shot to stardom in the early 1970s. A Beetle with very much a mind of his own, Herbie adopts a bewildered racing-driver owner and helps him to victory against all odds. Even when torn in two at the start of a race, Herbie manages to come in first and third. The real-life Herbie was heavily modified to perform its hair-raising stunts, with a Porsche engine and brakes, and he was driven by a back-seat driver crouched behind a screen.

Real Beetles have appeared in numerous other films. Diane Keaton drove one in *Annie Hall*. Woody Allen must have felt an affinity for such a modest, unassuming car as the Beetle, because it features again in another of his films, *Sleeper*. Transported 200 years into the future, Woody encounters a Beetle entombed in a cave. It starts, of course, at the first touch.

Just what is it about the humble Beetle that has inspired such enthusiasm? That kept people buying it, long after its contemporaries were rusting dead and forgotten in the scrapyard of automotive history? That turned this humble motor car into an icon of 20th century popular culture?

There's no one simple answer. Cheapness, reliability and economy all helped, of course. A more expensive car might be much admired, but its exclusivity would keep it from being part of a truly popular culture. The Beetle's reliability won it many long-term friends. Its quirkiness – its rear-engine, air-cooled configuration and its distinctive styling – helped it to stand out from the mass of everyday cars and gave it a sense of character and personality that few other cars could approach.

Perhaps the Beetle's looks established its main claim to people's affections. Though it's often been accused of being

Brighten up your Beetle

Beetle owners have always enjoyed giving their characterful cars even more of an individual identity. A vast number and variety of aftermarket accessories have been available over the years. After a slow start Volkswagen began making accessories itself, but it was independent companies who always seemed to come up with the most innovative, useful and downright off-beat.

First off the mark was an ex-Volkswagen employee called Karl Meier, who formed the Kamei company specializing in Beetle accessories. Ironically, Meier got his start directly because of Nordhoff's tough policy of restricting the sale of Beetle chassis to coachbuilders. This put out of business a firm called Schwen, who up till then had been making a variety of utilities, racing cars and even a coupé, all based on the Beetle chassis. Schwen was left with a large stock of unwanted Beetle seats.

Meier agreed to take these seats off Schwen's hands. He then re-upholstered them in natty 'salt and pepper' fabric, and sold them to VW dealers who used them to smarten up old Beetles. This venture proved profitable, and Meier's next idea, seat covers, went down even better. Soon there was a rear luggage compartment cover to add to the Kamei range, then cushions for neck, knee and arm, a dashboard shelf, a foot-rest and a waste paper bin.

Meier used to send out his young sons with leaflets advertising the latest Kamei accessory, to place on the windscreens of Beetles in the VW factory staff car park. If there was a healthy demand for the product among Volkswagen workers, Meier would go ahead and market it more widely.

Some of Kamei's accessories addressed obvious shortcomings in the Beetle. For instance, there was the extension for the reserve fuel tap which allowed it to be operated easily by hand. Many of Kamei's ideas later appeared on the Beetle as standard fittings. These included the conventional flat accelerator pedal that replaced the original roller ball variety, seat headrests and a glovebox.

One innovative item that was just too far ahead of its time was the Kamei spoiler, designed to fit under the Beetle's front bumper. Meier fashioned this from aluminium alloy with the help of an aircraft engineer, the aim being to reduce the Beetle's tendency to wander at motorway speeds and in sidewinds. Aerodynamically it was a great success – driving a Beetle equipped with his spoiler to the 1953 Geneva Motorshow, Meier appreciated the positive effect it had on his car's straightline stability. However, it had a decidedly negative effect on the crowds of Beetle owners at the show, and Meier reluctantly had to scrap the idea.

Popular period accessories in the 1950s included a fan (left), a gearlever ashtray (bottom left) and a steering-wheel clock and dashboard flower vase (bottom right)

When spoilers did become fashionable in the 1970s, Kamei launched a plastic chin spoiler which this time found wide acceptance among Beetle owners.

Numerous other firms also supplied accessories for the Beetle. Among the more interesting ideas were a fan to keep the interior cool, a gear-stick ashtray for smokers, and a choice of attractive dashboard flower vases in porcelain, steel or glass. Numerous fog and spot lamps were available to supplement the Beetle's lethargic headlamps, and one company, Helphos, even produced a searchlight. Mounted on the windscreen, it was ideal for illuminating poorly lit signposts.

All sorts of chrome add-ons were offered to beautify the Beetle's bodywork, including the popular headlamp 'eyelids', which give the Beetle an enticingly sultry air. They do nothing for its aerodynamics, though, and in Germany they were outlawed as a hazard to pedestrians. Another oddity was the spindly steel rods designed to be attached to the base of each wing, where by scraping along the kerb they acted as a primitive kind of parking radar.

The Beetle's traditionally spartan dashboard always presented a challenge to accessory fans, and there was never any shortage of supplementary gauges on offer to help liven it up. A fuel gauge was a popular option during the long years when the Beetle lacked this basic facility, and companies such as the British tuning firm Speedwell sold a whole range of rev counters, oil temperature and pressure gauges to enable you to keep a closer eye on your engine's health.

Nowadays, most of these original accessories are hard to find, but items like the Speedwell gauges have been remanufactured. Genuine or repro, period accessories are still much appreciated by enthusiasts looking to add a touch of extra character to their Beetle.

Turning your Beetle into a Water Bug has been a popular pastime, especially in the US. The pursuit isn't as difficult as it looks – the door seals in a Beetle are so good that even a standard Beetle will float, but not indefinitely!

So how many people can you squeeze into a Beetle? One team of rock-climbers managed fifty-seven...

bug-ugly, the Beetle does possess a recognizably happy, friendly face. Designers are well aware that cars, with their two headlamp 'eyes' and grille 'mouth' can easily be given human expressions. But in most cases, they design this expression to look what advertising copywriters call 'purposeful' – which usually just means aggressive.

In contrast, the Beetle's honest, cheerful, down-to-earth features are completely devoid of aggression. It has always appealed to easy-going types who don't

want to own a car that screams *getouttamyway* at every other driver on the road.

BEETLE TUNING

Not that this should be taken to imply that Beetle drivers always want to drive slowly. As many have discovered, one way to get a lot of fun out of their car is to give it decidedly more power than VW ever intended. Over the years the Beetle has spawned a

Beetles in motorsport

Old-fashioned, slow, with a low-revving engine and tricky rear-engined handling – anyone could see that the Beetle was never meant for motor racing. This was certainly the attitude Volkswagen took under Heinrich Nordhoff, who saw racing as a frivolous diversion from the Beetle's serious task of transporting people from A to B. Ferdinand Porsche, on the other hand, had been less strait-laced, as he showed when he threw himself enthusiastically into the task of building the Beetle-based Berlin–Rome racer of 1939.

And, as it turned out, the Beetle actually put up a surprisingly good showing in motorsport – once it had found its niche. Finding that niche meant taking a good look at the Beetle's strengths: excellent traction, ruggedness and manoeuvrability. These gave it an enormous advantage in events which involved loose surfaces, confined spaces and harsh conditions – in other words, rallying and autotests.

A Beetle was entered in the first postwar Monte Carlo rally, held in 1949, and came 43rd out of 166 entrants, and sixth in the under-1,500cc class – not bad for a first attempt. Beetles showed how tough they were in overseas events such as the African Safari Rally, won outright by Beetles in 1953, '54, '57 and '62. Rally ace Paddy Hopkirk learnt his trade in Ireland in a split-window Beetle, and Kevin Sherry ruffled a few feathers when his Beetle finished first in the 1959 Circuit of Ireland Rally, beating the works Triumph entrants.

Later on, Austrian VW importer Porsche Salzburg prepared Group 2 Beetles for the top international rallies. Their 1,600cc engines were tuned to thump out 126bhp, courtesy of two Weber twin-choke carbs, reprofiled camshafts, dry-sump engine lubrication, Mahle pistons, larger inlet valves and polished ports. They enjoyed several good years, and at their best took sixth place overall on the Swedish Rally and fifth on the Acropolis.

Beetles shone especially brightly in autotests, which involved lots of stops, starts and turns in tight spaces. With its rear-weight bias, the Beetle had a real advantage. In skilled hands, its natural propensity to oversteer could be used to make it change direction sharply, and the ease with which the Beetle would perform front and rear spin turns meant it literally ran rings round the opposition.

In America, the Beetle's exceptional strength led in the late 1960s to the development of a new sporting derivative: the Baja Bug. These rugged creatures were designed for the most punishing sort of off-road racing, over harsh desert courses of loose sand, rocks and gullies. Baja Bug bodies are cut away and raised to allow steep slopes to be tackled without grounding, and metal plates protect the underside. Engines are enlarged to two litres or more and huge knobbly tyres are fitted. Glass-melting headlamps are needed, for the races are often run overnight, when the dangers can be considerable.

It was in America that another use was found for the Beetle's excellent traction: to help it off the mark on the dragstrip. Beetles first started turning up on dragstrips in the early 1960s, much to the amusement of other drivers in their souped-up big V8 saloons. But with the increasing availability of tuning parts, and its great traction allied to its light weight, the Beetle started surprising everybody by consistently winning its class.

All-Beetle drag races (known as Bug-ins) became popular in the US, while the top competitors began developing some seriously quick Beetle-based dragsters. 'Inch Pincher', run by tuning specialist EMPI, made the opposition sit up and take notice, turning in quarter mile times around 15sec/91mph (146km/h) in the mid-1960s. Today's 'funny cars' feature a glassfibre Beetle bodyshell that often hides most un-Beetle-like running gear, and the best are capable of topping 150mph (240km/h) over the quarter mile.

Meanwhile, the Beetle made its appearance on the racetrack, in the form of Formula Vee. This budget single-seater racing formula had its origins in 1961 when a Miami VW dealer, Hubert

The Beetle's excellent traction, toughness and manoeuvrability made it the natural choice as the basis for purpose-built off-road desert racers. This bucking bronco is tackling the challenging Baja 1000 in Mexico.

'Outrage' is the top Beetle drag racer, holding the world record for VW funny cars. Powered by an incredible turbocharged, methanol-fuelled, 750bhp 2.8-litre flat-four, it's capable of a 7.7sec/161mph (258 km/h) quarter-mile.

Brundage, commissioned a VW-powered racer to use in US Formula Junior races. Thanks to its relative cheapness and the easy availability of spares, the idea of basing a single-seater on the Beetle caught on. Porsche's racing manager, Huschke von Hanstein, came across the Formula Vee racers on a trip to America, took up the concept enthusiastically and began promoting it in Europe, where it is still going strong today.

In the UK, Formula Vee cars are based around the 1300 single-port engine, modified to produce up to 95bhp, with the familiar Beetle torsion bar suspension with swing axles at the rear. Regulations are kept tight, which means that the action is close and drivers don't need to invest vast amounts of cash to achieve success.

Formula Vee racers dice at Daytona in 1966. These Beetle-powered single-seaters quickly spread in popularity and established themselves in Europe as a cheap, competitive and thrilling race series. Formula Vee racing is still going strong today.

Also designed to give exciting, closely matched, racing is the Käfer cup, which began in Germany in 1989, and spread to the UK as the Beetle Cup in 1992. The Beetles look more or less standard, but modifications are allowed to the engines within strict limits. They're taken out to 1,641cc, sports camshafts are fitted along with a 40mm dellorto carburettor and an uprated oil pump, suspension is lowered and stiffened, and a sports seat, fire extinguisher and roll cage installed. With around 70bhp on tap, speeds can approach 100mph (160km/h) and the action is fast and furious.

Most importantly, in a racing scene where costs can be frightening if you want to be competitive, the Beetle Cup gives the chance for those on a limited budget to compete on equal terms with the better-funded. Just like it did on the roads, the Beetle has brought a much-appreciated dose of egalitarianism to the world of motorsport.

massive tuning industry, offering a vast range of go-faster equipment to satisfy all tastes, from the driver who'd just like a bit more pulling power up the hills, to hot-rodders who want to squeeze enough perfor-mance from their Beetles to outgun a Porsche 911.

This industry developed in the face of one obvious drawback – that the Beetle is not the most likely candidate for perfor-

An extraordinary variety of models of the Beetle have been made over the years. Early and rare examples are now highly sought-after, and make valuable collector's items.

Walt Disney's Love Bug *captured cinema-goers' hearts in the 1970s. VW weren't slow to recognize the film's promotional virtues and dressed up a few Herbie-lookalikes of their own.*

mance tuning. Its flat-four engine was designed with reliability as the top priority. Power output was actually restricted by the long inlet manifolds and small single carburettor, which restricted the breathing of the engine so that it was near-impossible to cause damage by over-revving. These safeguards could be overcome – an obvious tuning route was to fit new carbs and inlet manifolds – but the extra power liberated then put more stress on other parts of the engine that were never designed to cope with it. Tuning, as enthusiasts discovered, was an exercise to be undertaken only with considerable caution and expertise.

Volkswagen itself was no help, maintaining its puritanical view that the Beetle was meant to be practical transport, not a

Volkswagen's promotional material didn't fail to appreciate the Beetle's cheeky appeal.

sports car. If you wanted a sports car, buy a Porsche instead. VW endowed the Beetle with the bare minimum of power that most drivers would need. They never offered a true sporting version of the Beetle – even the GT special edition featured the standard 1600 engine – and only in Brazil and South Africa were official Beetle models available with twin carburettors.

This left the way open for independent specialists to meet the demand for tuning. Even in the 1950s there was a healthy and growing interest in tuning. Many owners enjoyed their Beetles, but reckoned they'd enjoy them even more if they had a bit more oomph. Right up until 1966 the Beetle was only available with a 1200 engine. With no more than 34bhp to play with, the resulting performance – little more than 70mph (110km/h) flat out, and 0-60mph (100km/h) in around 28 seconds – was sluggish even by the standards of the day.

One of the first – and most successful – of the Beetle tuning companies was Okrasa. Okrasa's first conversion was for the 1,131c engine, and they offered two stages of tuning to choose from. The cheaper and simpler stage involved replacing the existing cylinder heads with heads purpose-designed by Okrasa. The Okrasa heads featured twin inlet ports for better breathing, larger valves, and they were matched to a pair of Solex 32PBI carburettors. They increased power by around a third, which was a significant gain in performance terms, and it turned the Beetle into an altogether more sprightly mover.

For a real transformation, though, the second stage was the business. This involved a more thorough reworking of the engine. Its capacity was taken out to 1,293cc by fitting a forged longer-stroke crankshaft, the Stage One cylinder heads and hotter camshafts, and the resulting power output increased to 48bhp.

What made Okrasa's products stand out was the quality of the engineering, which meant that not only could you improve engine performance, you could do it without having to cross your fingers that the whole thing wouldn't go bang 2,000 miles down the road. In fact, Okrasa (now renamed Oettinger) was unique in being the only tuning company to receive official VW approval.

The taste for modifying the Beetle spread rapidly, with tuning firms springing up wherever the Beetle was sold to cater for local demand. Tuning caught on in a big way in America, where a company called EMPI led the way. EMPI started out in 1956 producing replacement valve guides, which allowed owners to repair worn Beetle cylinder heads that previously would have had to be scrapped. The move into tuning was a natural step. One of EMPI's most successful innovations was their camber compensator, which attached to the rear suspension and reduced the Beetle's tendency to oversteer.

EMPI also marketed the Okrasa tuning kits, and in time developed extra engine tuning modifications of their own. By the late 1960s they were offering a complete modified Beetle package – the GTV. This was available in four stages of tune, with the GTV MkIV featuring uprated shock absorbers, a front anti-roll bar, the rear camber compensator, 5.5in Porsche-style wheels and lots of extra chrome and stripes. With a big-bore cylinder barrel conversion upping capacity to 1,688cc, the GTV produced an impressive 75–80bhp.

Back in Europe in the 1950s, several companies began offering a similar conversion to the Okrasa one. Denzel in Austria fitted a longer-stroke crankshaft and bigger pistons to achieve a capacity of 1,281cc. With the familiar pair of Solex 32PBIs

added, this was good for around 48bhp and a claimed 93mph (149km/h) top speed.

In England, Tarrant and Frazer offered a comparatively simple twin-carb conversion, which involved adding an extra Solex carburettor to the existing one. This had the benefit of being a simple modification to carry out, which kept costs down: fitted, it added just £48 to the £740 cost of a new Beetle. *Autosport*, testing a modified Tarrant and Frazer car in 1955, found that it ran rings round the standard model, cutting the 0–60mph time to 25sec. Although it was hardly neck-snapping, it was a lot livelier than the standard car, which had trouble reaching 60mph in twice that time.

Supercharging was another tuning method that appealed for its simplicity. Judson in America offered a kit that simply bolted on to the engine, which needed no internal modifications. The blower was driven by a belt off the crankshaft pulley, and boosted power to similar levels as the Okrasa conversion, cutting the 0–60mph time to under sixteen seconds. Whether increasing power this way was in the long term as reliable a solution as the Okrasa route was less certain.

One other tempting option for the home tuner was to replace the standard engine with the one used in the Porsche 356. This model started out using a little-modified version of the Beetle's flat-four, which was soon replaced by a bored-out 1,286cc unit and then, in 1951, a yet more powerful 1,488cc, 55bhp version. Other Porsche suspension and brake parts remained a useful weapon in the tuner's armoury for many years to come. The finned brake drums from the 356 were particularly popular with owners keen to avoid the fade which stock items were prone to when used hard.

The arrival of the bigger 1,285cc engine in 1966 made most of the traditional engine conversions redundant. In the well worn phrase, there's no substitute for cubic inches, and fitting a 1300 engine was a more effective way to improve performance than tweaking a 1200 unit. Of course, no sooner had the 1300 arrived than tuners started to turn their attention to that unit, only to be trumped again when VW launched the 1500 the following year. That engine, in turn, could always be replaced by a 1600, the largest engine to find its way officially into the Beetle.

But the options didn't end there. As other models expanded the Volkswagen range, it didn't take enthusiasts long to consider the possibility of using their versions of the flat-four in the Beetle. When the 1600-engined Type 3 arrived, its 54bhp twin-carb engine offered a useful improve-

ment over what the Beetle had to offer. The only problem was that the cooling system of this engine needed modifying extensively before it would fit the Beetle.

The same problem applied to the Type 4 engine, a more powerful and robust re-engineered version of the Beetle's flat-four, which, in fuel-injected form, produces 80bhp. This engine is also a much better starting point for tuning, and has been enlarged to 2.7 litres and 200bhp for use in racing Beetles. It's a tight fit in the Beetle's engine bay, however, and the job entails revamping the cooling system, preferably by fitting a Porsche 911 cooling fan.

The Type 2 also had something to offer. Some enthusiasts have fitted the 1.9-litre engine fitted to the later Type 2 models.

Once a really serious tuner has gone to work on it, you'll hardly recognize the Beetle's flat-four.

With 78bhp, this provides the Beetle with more than enough oomph, the only drawback being that this version of the flat-four is water-cooled, which means it detracts too much from the Beetle's original character for most owners' tastes.

But if it's serious high performance you're after, originality does have to take a back seat. One German dealership in the 1970s produced a Porsche 911-engined Beetle. The 2.7-litre flat-six engine, producing 210bhp, had to be mounted amidships, and was accompanied by suspension from the VW-Porsche 914. The resulting 125mph (200km/h) Beetle was finished to such a high standard that it actually met stringent German TÜV regulations for use on public roads. Over the years customizers have fitted Beetles with all sorts of

unlikely power units – some have managed to build V8-powered Beetles – even if it means having to turn the Beetle inside out by relocating the engine in the front.

BEETLE CUSTOMIZING

Alongside the craze for making your Beetle go faster, there has always been a whole separate discipline of making it look better. Many Beetle enthusiasts would argue, of course, that the classic lines of Ferdinand Porsche's original design are impossible to improve upon. But as long as owners have loved their Beetles, they've felt the urge to make their car stand out from the crowd.

Like Beetle tuning, Beetle customizing ultimately became big business. The most

Beetle tuners go to incredible lengths to extract more power from their cars, but few Beetles are as extreme as this one. Instead of the usual flat-four, it's been fitted with a 3.5-litre Rover V8 engine.

171

This shot of an authentic Orange Country Cal-looker shows how subtle lowering and style modifications can result in a Beetle that is both distinctive and tasteful (except for the furry dice, that is).

famous school of Beetle customizing, which became known as the California-look (abbreviated to Cal-look), was popularized on the West Coast of America in the mid-1970s. Its origins go back a little further, to a Beetle-tuning club called Der Kleiner Panzers. One member, Greg Aronson, stripped the body trim from his 1963 Beetle, including the bumpers, had the resulting bolt holes welded up, and resprayed the car white. He lowered the front suspension, dropped in a tuned engine, and finished everything off with a set of EMPI wheels. The Cal-look was born.

It took a while to catch on, but gradually more and more Beetles appeared with the clean, uncluttered, bodywork and lowered suspension that characterized the look. The suspension modifications, inci-

dentally, were there for looks rather than performance, and often ended up making the car handle worse, not better.

For those who didn't appreciate the Cal-look, there were plenty of alternatives. Beetles could be modified with cut-back wings, bonnet and boot to echo the styling of the Baja bugs that competed in the famous Baja 1000 off-road races in the south-west of America. Or, a completely new glassfibre body could be transplanted to form a Beach Buggy. With seats open to the elements, Buggys were ideally suited to the Californian climate, and they provided a simple way to rejuvenate a tatty, but mechanically sound Beetle. A wide variety of other glassfibre bodies have been dreamed up for the Beetle over the years, recalling the coachbuilt specials of the

1950s in spirit, if not always in taste.

As a visit to any of the many Beetle shows held each year will reveal, customized Beetles are still extremely popular. Nowadays, however, there's a greater emphasis on preserving the originality of older and rarer Beetles, and a nice compromize has emerged in the Resto-Cal-look, which applies subtle elements of the Cal-look to restored older Beetles. The enjoyment which enthusiasts have had over the years from tuning and customizing their cars adds an intriguing extra dimension to the history of this most versatile of cars, and today an early Cal-looker or period-tuned Beetle is a collector's item in its own right.

Even Volkswagen got in on the modified Beetle act – the above conversion took visitors on factory tours, while the Beetle train (right) toured Wolfburg for some two decades during which it carried 130,000 visitors.

173

You want a really unusual Beetle? How about a Beetle limousine, or a Beetle Rolls-Royce convertible?

Bizarre uses for a Beetle No.437. This ex-Baja Bug left its exciting days of tearing across the desert behind, and settled down to a peaceful retirement spent farming in the country.

10   Buying a Beetle

Of the 21,300,000 Beetles built over the last half century, a healthy number remain on the road, thanks partly to the fact that the car was built to last, and partly to the efforts of Beetle owners to look after their cars.

A prospective Beetle owner is in a much better position than most classic car buyers. Because Beetles are plentiful, you can afford to be choosy and wait for the right car to come along. If you need help, there are a wealth of specialists and owners' clubs ready with friendly advice and information. So many people have spent so much time doing so many things with Beetles, that even if you want to try something out of the ordinary, like an exotic engine transplant, there's bound to be someone who has tried it first and will be only too pleased to help steer you round any problems you encounter.

Other good news is that, thanks to the Beetle's enduring popularity, spare parts are generally easy to find and competitively priced. Old stock is still available from VW dealers, numerous specialists have manufactured their own, usually cheaper, parts, and continuing production in Mexico and Brazil means brand new parts can be obtained from the VW factories there.

But which Beetle to choose? Split or oval, 1200 or 1600, torsion bar or MacPherson strut? The Beetle may not have altered much to look at over its fifty years of production, but as we've seen, changes were continuously made throughout its life, and these need considering carefully if you're to find the Beetle best suited to your tastes.

Part of the appeal of a classic car is precisely that it's a few years old – maybe as old as yourself, or even older. Such a car will have picked up a fascinating history through its long life. Inevitably, older models are rarer, more sought-after and more expensive – in the case of the Beetle, the older split- and oval-window models are particularly appreciated because in styling and specification they remain so faithful to Ferdinand Porsche's original design.

With each successive production change, the Beetle departed further from the purity of its original design. Enthusiasts sometimes regard a certain point as marking the end of the 'real' Beetle – say, the introduction of twelve-volt electrics, the switch to upright headlamps or the adoption of MacPherson strut front suspension. It all depends on your personal viewpoint. Others would consider a Beetle a Beetle, whether it's a 1956 Oval or a 1996 Mexican. But you need to balance the undoubted appeal of the older cars against the very real consideration that with each passing year the Beetle became more practical, easy to live with and better-suited to today's driving conditions.

So if you intend buying a Beetle, first you must consider exactly what you intend doing with it. If you want to use it every day, commuting on motorways and driving it in the depths of winter, then unless you want to make life really interesting for yourself, you'll be better off with a later model. If you just intend using your car on the occasional summer weekend then your choice can be much wider.

Being so sought-after, early cars, the splits and increasingly the ovals, carry a price premium. Few see use as everyday cars. Features like cable brakes, semaphore indicators and crash gearboxes mean that it takes skill and experience to drive an early Beetle well, and they demand extra care on today's fast and busy roads. Early cars also have the link-pin front

An early Oval, or a 1303 Cabriolet? The choice of Beetles is a wide one. Each version has its own set of advantages and drawbacks, which you need to take into consideration before buying a Beetle.

suspension, and parts for this can be hard to find (it was replaced in 1966 by a ball-joint set-up).

Later cars have better all-round visibility and a higher level of safety equipment. Items to consider, and the model years in which they arrived, are: flashing indicators (1961); front seat belt anchorage points (1962); anti-burst door locks (1966); hazard warning lights (1966); dual-circuit brakes (1968); and collapsible steering column (1968). From 1968 the Beetle also has twelve-volt electrics, which mean brighter lights and better starting on cold mornings.

Handling is an aspect of the Beetle that attracted a lot of criticism over the years, but it's less important to today's buyer. Beetle owners generally drive at a pace that respects their car's age, and even in an earlier model aren't likely to exceed the limits of roadholding. However, if you do like to press on, aren't experienced with rear-wheel-drive, and have no great wish to learn how to control a tail slide the hard way, then a 1967 or later Beetle is best for you.

This was the year when the equalizer spring was fitted to the rear suspension, minimizing camber changes and reducing the likelihood of the tail breaking loose. Ultimately, the double-jointed rear axles, first seen on the semi-automatic and standardized on the 1302 and 1303, deliver the most foolproof Beetle handling. At the front, there's little in the way of any handling advantage to be gained by the MacPherson strut suspension which replaced traditional torsion bars in the 1302 and 1303 Super Beetles, but it does give these models a clear advantage in luggage capacity.

Rapid performance isn't a number one consideration when buying a Beetle – even the quicker models are slower than a modern supermini – but engine size is still worth thinking about. With just 34bhp to play with, 1,200cc cars can feel sluggish.

On the other hand, the twin-port 1300 and 1600 engines are susceptible to flat-spots, and are a lot less fuel-efficient. The Super Beetles carry an extra weight penalty, and really need the 1600 engine if they're to provide decent progress. Quickest (and hence among the most popular) Beetle models are the 1500 and the GT special edition.

Tuning the Beetle has been so popular that you're quite likely to come across a 1300 Beetle that's been fitted with, say, a 1,500cc engine. Or, for that matter, a 1966 car fitted with twelve-volt electrics, or even a split-window Beetle that has at some stage in its past been fitted with an oval rear window in the interests of better visibility.

Such modifications add to the practicality of an earlier car, but whether you'll be tempted to purchase it depends on your attitude to originality. A truly original car should have only genuine VW parts fitted, and no changes to the way it looked when it left the factory. If you intend to get involved in the concours scene, returning your car to pristine condition and entering it at shows, then its originality will be paramount for you, and you should go over a prospective purchase with a fine-tooth comb to ensure that everything is exactly how it should be.

On the other hand, a highly modified Beetle can be great fun. The customizing scene is still going strong, and there are so many custom Beetles around that it's easy to buy an already modified Beetle – if a lot less entertaining than doing the work for yourself. If you take this route, it does pay to have a professional take a careful look at the quality of the work that's been carried out before handing over the cheque.

In fact, whatever Beetle model you

Club life

Beetles generate such an enormous degree of loyalty and enthusiasm that it's no surprise that Beetle clubs have been formed all over the world, creating a social focus for owners to meet and share their experience and love of this unique motor car.

The distinction of being the first country to form such a club goes to Britain, where John Colborne-Baber, the Surrey motor dealer who first sold Beetles in the late 1940s, set up a VW Owners Club in 1953. Interestingly, it was this club which popularized the used of the name 'Beetle' for the car, which at that time was known simply as the Volkswagen – the club magazine

VW dealer John Colborne-Baber set up the first VW owners club, calling its magazine Beetling *after the nickname his son's school-friends gave his car. These shots were taken at one of the club's first meetings held in 1953.*

was called *Beetling*.

The Beetle nickname was bestowed by schoolboy friends of Colborne-Baber's son, Peter. He recalls 'My father used to come to my school to pick me up after football matches. The boys would see him drive up behind the school bus in his VW, which was an unusual sight in those days, and they used to shout out "Here comes Baber in his Beetle!". That was the first time the name was ever used.'

Since those early days the club has expanded dramatically and established many regional branches. Numerous other clubs have also been founded. Some cater for particular years or models, while others bring together owners of customized or racing Beetles, or of Beetle-derived vehicles such as the Karmann Ghia and Types 2, 3 and 4. These clubs are invaluable for the owner as a source of information, spares, advice and discounts, as well as for their lively social scene.

Beetle clubs now exist across the world, from Finland to New Zealand. In countries where the Beetle was actually produced the following is, of course, that much more enthusiastic. In Indonesia, for instance, where Beetles were made from 1972-76, there are some 20 VW groups. In 1993 the Bali division celebrated their second birthday with a rally of over 300 Beetles, some of which drove more than 1,000kms (600 miles) to take part.

Where the Beetle is still being produced, enthusiasm runs even higher. In Brazil, where the Beetle is called the Fusca, local 'Fuscamaniacs' once put together a record-breaking convoy of over 1,500 VWs.

---

decide on, it's an excellent idea to get your prospective purchase checked over by someone who knows exactly what they're looking for. Most local owners' clubs have knowledgeable enthusiasts who will be happy to help you make the right decision – and clubs are also a good place to find honest Beetles for sale.

Alternatively, you can ask a reputable specialist to carry out an inspection on a car you're thinking of buying. This service often comes cheaper than you'd expect, because specialists see it as a good way to win your future custom.

Most Beetle sellers may be honest and straight with you, but there are still a lot of cars out there that have been tarted up to look better than they really are, or which are on the verge of needing large sums of money spent on them. A thorough inspection, including a long test drive, is vital to avoid making an expensive mistake. What follows is a brief guide to the main troublespots to look out for when examining a Beetle.

BODYWORK

The Beetle earned an enviable reputation for defying corrosion, remaining in sound bodily condition for years after its competitors had rusted into the ground. While this certainly was the case, Beetles purchased today have generally had a long time for rust to sink its teeth into them.

It's a lot easier to bodge up rusted areas and hide them, at least for as long as it takes to sell a car, than to get them properly repaired, so it's vital to keep an eye open not only for the obvious signs of rusting but also for clues as to where it might have been covered up. These include suspicious-looking plates welded onto the chassis, or ripples in the bodywork which may indicate where filler has been used (running a magnet over the area will soon confirm this).

Interestingly, although early Beetles did deserve their reputation for resisting rust, those built in the 1970s have fared much less well, possibly due to a deterioration in

Which Beetle?

Model	For	Against
Split/Oval 1200	Full of character; original looks; mostly cherished, well-maintained cars; economical	Rare, expensive to buy; some trim can be hard to find; slow; not practical for everyday use
Later 1200	Retains more of original Beetle character than larger-engined models; economical	Slow; lacks creature comforts; few safety features; handling can be tricky; six-volt electrics
1300	Decent performance; handles well; looks good	Fewer safety features than later Super Beetles
1500	Surprisingly nippy, handles well; better brakes; looks good	Fewer safety features than later Super Beetles
1302/1303	Comfortable; good visibility; high specification; extra luggage space; lots of safety features;	More expensive to run than earlier models; heavier and slower than single-port 1300; less-appealing styling
1302S/1303S	Comfortable; good visibility; high specification; extra luggage space; lots of safety features; good brakes	More expensive to run than earlier models; 1600 engine is thirsty; less appealing styling
Cabriolet	Good looks; style; a truly practical convertible	Expensive to buy; some dodgy examples on sale

the quality of steel used at that time.

Whereabouts the corrosion has set in is the important question. Bonnets can be replaced fairly cheaply, and the wings, which bolt on, can easily be removed and replaced. However, if rust has seriously attacked the door pillars, the base of the windscreen, or the floorpan, the repair bill starts getting expensive. Doing a decent job of repairing advanced corrosion in these areas will entail removing the body from the chassis.

Check also for signs of rust on the shock absorber top mounting points, which is an MoT failure point. Rust around the Mac-Pherson strut mounting points of a 1302 or 1303 is a particularly serious matter.

It's important to investigate the sills for signs of rust, as these not only attach the body to the floorpan, but also channel air into the car as part of the heating system. One sign of defective sills is to turn the heater on during the test drive – if the air flow is poor, then they're likely to be holed. A poor heater may also point to faulty heat exchangers, which are costly to replace.

On the chassis itself, one area that's commonly affected by rust is under the back seat around the battery. Lift the seat to check this, and then look under the mats for signs of rust on the rest of the floorpan. Check the spare wheel well under the front bonnet too.

Even if rust is terminally advanced, it's

not necessarily a disaster. Replacement glassfibre bodies and even whole steel bodyshells are available from specialists.

RUNNING GEAR

The Beetle's flat-four is renowned for its ruggedness and longevity. This reputation was well deserved. However . . .

The 'however' is that while the engine was certainly reliable by comparison to those found in other popular 1950s cars, this doesn't mean you can expect it to have the same reliability as a modern production engine. And although the Beetle engine was improved and strengthened during its development, it also underwent a series of increases in capacity and power output which had a detrimental effect on its durability. While it is true to say that an 1,192cc Beetle engine could be run flat-out on the motorway all day long with no adverse effects, this is less true of the later, larger-capacity units.

Something else to bear in mind is that the reliability of a Beetle engine is closely linked to the quality of maintenance it has received. Because the engine depends on its oil not only for lubrication, but also for cooling, running it with old, dirty oil rapidly destroys it. This is particularly so because right up till 1993 on the latest Mexican Beetles, the engine lacked a proper oil filter. Beetle engines need their oil changed religiously every 2,000 miles, and letting a Beetle run low on oil is a far more serious matter than it is with most cars.

The oil should ideally be an old-fashioned 30-grade monograde type. Unlike most cars, the Beetle has a pressure valve instead of a thermostat in its oil cooling system. Modern multigrade oils, which are designed to retain their viscosity at high temperatures, may delay the operation of the oil cooler and lead to overheating. However, now that monograde oil is getting harder to find, many owners are swapping

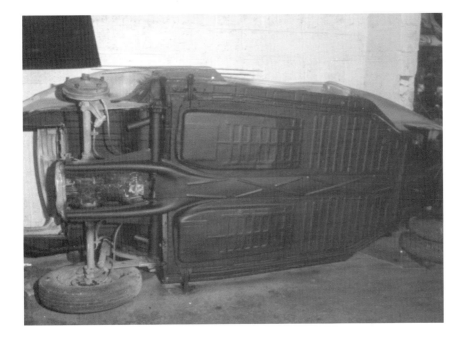

The Beetle's separate chassis/floorpan can be unbolted to allow access to corroded chassis or body panels – rust commonly attacks the chassis under the back seat and in the spare wheel well.

181

Damaged wings are also easy to unbolt and replace if necessary.

If chassis corrosion is not too far advanced, patches can be cut out and new metal welded in.

182

Valve clearances should be checked regularly, or overheating and valve damage can occur.

A Beetle engine is less tricky to rebuild than most, and parts are generally easy to find and inexpensive.

to reputable 15/40W oils with no detrimental effects.

The engine also needs its valve clearances checked regularly – ideally at the same 2,000-mile intervals. Incorrect clearances can lead to the exhaust valves running too hot, and this will ultimately cause valve failure.

If these simple tasks are neglected then the lifespan of a Beetle engine is likely to be drastically reduced. When considering the purchase of a Beetle, it's equally important to examine its owner. Find out how much the owner knows about his or her car,

The Beetle's rugged gearbox rarely goes wrong – but when it does, it needs professional attention.

and whether they've been carrying out the proper maintenance.

Before starting the engine, take a good look at the fan housing to ensure it is correctly fitted, and that there are no seals missing – this could cause air to leak out, reducing the fan's efficiency and leading to overheating.

On starting the engine, don't be alarmed if you see a small puff of smoke from the exhaust – this is feature of the flat-four's horizontal design, and is caused by oil seeping into the combustion chambers while at rest, particularly if the car is parked on a slope. However, any further emissions of smoke are a definite warning sign.

Being air-cooled, the Beetle engine is naturally quite loud, but the noise should be a healthy tappetty sound. Listen out for

grinding, rumbling, rattling and knocking which may indicate heavy wear.

If wear is present, the good news is that a Beetle engine can be rebuilt fairly cheaply. If the car is otherwise in good condition it may still be worth buying – just budget for the extra expense, and use it to bargain down the asking price.

The Beetle's gearbox fully deserves a reputation for unburstability. Gearchanges should be quick, light and precise. If you do encounter a 'box that has weak synchromesh, or jumps out of gear, it needs the attention of a specialist and repairs will probably be costly.

The semi-automatic transmission has something of an undeserved reputation for being troublesome, as in properly maintained cars it is generally pretty reliable.

Fitting high-quality new shock absorbers can transform the handling of a tired Beetle.

Problems with gearchanging may just be due to faulty or dirty microswitches at the base of the gear lever.

BRAKES AND SUSPENSION

Beetles equipped with drum brakes should stop perfectly adequately, but this does depend on the drums being in good order. Make sure the car pulls up in a straight line, and look for signs of oil leaking around the rear drums and contaminating the shoes. Quite a few cars which originally had front drums have since been fitted with discs.

A small amount of free-play in the steering (say a couple of centimetres at the rim in the straight-ahead position) can be

expected, but much more than this may indicate a worn steering box, which is expensive to put right, or worn ball-joints.

CABRIOLET

Beetle Cabriolets are highly sought-after and command much higher prices than the equivalent saloons. Consequently, it's even more worthwhile for an unscrupulous seller to bodge up a Cabriolet for a profit, and the buyer needs to be extra vigilant.

One hybrid to look out for is the saloon that has been turned into a convertible simply by chopping off its roof. As Karmann originally discovered, such an operation is only successful if it's accompanied by comprehensive strengthening of

185

When buying a Cabriolet, check that a high-quality hood is fitted. A proper, snug-fitting hood with its glass rear window makes the Cabriolet a quiet and practical vehicle to drive, summer or winter.

Some late-model Cabriolets have been imported from the US and these are fitted with fuel-injection. This can give trouble, and parts may be expensive and hard to find.

A restorer's dream! Split- and oval-window Beetles rarely turn up any more in this sort of condition.

the bodyshell. This is all too often skimped on chopped saloon cabriolets, and the result is a car that's creaky, rattly and not particularly enjoyable to drive. A cheap substitute hood also takes away much of the pleasure of driving a real Karmann Cabriolet, which should provide a genuinely quiet and refined, draughtless and leak-free experience.

As the chassis on the Cabriolet is heavily reinforced, rust has more places to strike and, if far advanced, can have a more serious effect on the structural integrity of the vehicle. Examine the underside with extra thoroughness.

When considering a specialized Beetle, such as an early model, a semi-auto or a Cabriolet, the best move is to join one of the owners' clubs which specialize in these models and can supply advice on avoiding the pitfalls involved in buying one.

RESTORATION

Restoration of any classic car is never a task to be undertaken lightly, but the Beetle offers several advantages.

Its construction, with a body that unbolts from the chassis, and wings that unbolt from the body, means that stripping the car down and replacing badly corroded wings is a relatively straightforward task. Thanks to the Beetle's popularity, repair panels and replacement parts are easy to come by and reasonably priced.

Rebuilding the engine is a job that can be confidently tackled without needing a vast amount of experience, and again there is a plentiful supply of parts available, and if necessary good-quality reconditioned engines can be bought.

Even obtaining replacement trim, which is often the trickiest part of restoring a classic car, isn't likely to pose a problem with the Beetle unless you're tackling a particularly old or unusual model.

Don't underestimate the hard labour and dedication that a restoration project entails, but if you do decide to go ahead, the reward of saving a Beetle from the scrapheap and preserving it for future generations to enjoy will certainly make your efforts well worthwhile.

11 Beetles Today – and Tomorrow

If you were hoping to buy yourself an immaculate Beetle, and reading the previous chapter about where they go wrong has left you feeling a little apprehensive, don't worry. You can always buy a brand new one.

Few people outside the world of Beetle enthusiasts realize that this incredible car is still in production, more than sixty years after Ferdinand Porsche first put its design to paper. In both Mexico and Brazil, citizens are eagerly purchasing the latest Sedan (as it's rather plainly known in Mexico), or Fusca (to give it its Brazilian title).

These Beetles didn't exactly take over where the German Beetle left off – they performed a neat sidestep, and each carried on in its own sweet way. This means they are an intriguing amalgamation of new and old.

The Mexican Beetle, for instance, features multi-point fuel injection, a three-way catalytic converter, an electric windscreen washer and rear seat belts, but it's still based on the old swing-axle rear suspension, and has less sound deadening material than the last German-built Beetles.

The Brazilian Fusca is generally less advanced than its Mexican cousin. It still uses the pre-1965 bodyshell with its narrower front and rear screens, though in combination with the later style wings with upright headlamps.

BRAZILIAN BEETLES

Brazil has had a particularly close relationship with the Beetle, being the first country outside Germany to set up a Beetle production plant. This came about through the efforts of one José Bastos Thompson, who was the Brazilian importer for Chrysler. Thompson realized that big inefficient motor cars like those Chrysler produced were not the answer to Brazil's needs. What was required was a car that was cheap to buy, reliable, rugged enough to cope with Brazil's network of poorly surfaced tracks, and economical on fuel to reduce the cost of imported oil. Ideally it would be built within Brazil to boost the country's balance of payments.

Thompson approached Heinrich Nordhoff, who visited Brazil accompanied by Wolfsburg colleague Friedrich Schultz-Wenk. Nordhoff was sufficiently impressed to give the go-ahead for an assembly plant – Schultz-Wenk was so taken by the country that he stayed to set up the operation, and ultimately took up Brazilian citizenship.

Volkswagen do Brasil was founded in March 1953, being eighty per cent funded by Wolfsburg. It began assembling Beetles from imported kits, and by 1956 it employed 200 workers and had put together 2,820 cars. This success encouraged the Brazilian government to step in and put forward finance for a plant that would

New Beetles (or 'Fuscas', as they're called) coming to life in Brazil. Continuing demand there for a small, cheap rugged car led to production of the Fusca restarting in 1993 after a seven-year gap.

The Brazilian Fusca is based on the torsion bar Beetle, with its upright spare wheel under the front bonnet. In 1994, a year after being reintroduced to Brazil, it was the country's twelfth best-selling car – not bad going for a sixty-year-old design.

manufacture rather than simply assemble Volkswagens.

Foundations for this plant were laid in 1956, and the following year the first Brazilian-manufactured VW, a Transporter, rolled off the production lines. In 1959 the plant began to build Beetles, which were fitted with lower compression engines and stronger suspensions to cope with local conditions.

The Beetle, or, we should say, Fusca, proved to be a spectacular success in Brazil. In 1962 it became the best-selling car there, and in March 1972 the millionth Fusca was made. Yearly sales in the early 1970s exceeded 200,000, and VW do Brasil became the country's largest industrial organization.

The company was active in other areas too, turning out a number of variations on

the VW theme. These included a four-door Type 3 saloon in 1971, and, the following year, the SP2, a sleek coupé with a 1,678cc engine. VW do Brasil had high hopes for exporting the SP2, but, in a bizarre oversight, its headlamps had been positioned too low to meet the legal requirements of most potential markets. After this came the Brasilia, a modern-looking two-door hatchback based on Beetle running gear, and later still the Gol (which means 'goal' in football-mad Brazil), which was essentially a German Golf fitted with a front-mounted 1300 Beetle engine.

Meanwhile, the Fusca was being exported to more than sixty countries. Like its European cousin, it had been updated continuously over the years, with a 1,300cc 46bhp engine arriving in 1967, twelve-volt electrics in 1968, and a 52bhp 1500 joining

VW do Brasil's sleek SP2 coupé of 1972 might have had the potential to sell worldwide, but its low headlamps infringed traffic rules in most countries, limiting sales to a few Middle-Eastern states.

A modern-looking hatchback based on Beetle running gear, the Brasilia sold well in Brazil from the mid-1970s to mid-1980s. A four-door version, sold in Nigeria, was badged the Igala.

191

One intriguing Brazilian hybrid was the Gol – essentially a Golf with a front-mounted Beetle engine.

the range in 1970. In 1973 the heating system became an optional extra (sensibly enough in the tropics), and the following year saw the introduction of the 1600S Super-Fuscão, fitted with a 65bhp twin-carb 1600 engine and featuring a three-spoke sports steering wheel, temperature gauge, clock and ammeter.

The two-millionth Fusca was built in 1976, and the following year saw a number of safety features fitted, including a collapsible steering column and dual-circuit brakes.

In 1983 the Fusca was limited to the 1300 engine and, in an effort to reduce dependence on imported fuel, an alcohol-burning version was introduced, running on fuel distilled from sugar-cane which

grows abundantly in Brazil. The following year, however, the 1300 was phased out in favour of the 1600 engine, which had undergone extensive modifications to provide more efficient combustion.

Then, at the end of 1986 and after 3.3 million had been produced, the Fusca was discontinued so that VW do Brasil could concentrate on its water-cooled models. This also meant the end of production in Nigeria, where Brazilian Beetles had been assembled from kits since 1975. It looked like the end of the road was approaching for the Beetle, which now hung on precariously in production in only one country – Mexico.

However, the obituaries proved to be premature. In August 1993 Autolatina (the holding company which oversees both VW and Ford in Brazil) resurrected the Fusca. They stressed its durability, economy, and ability to tackle all sorts of terrain in a country where less than ten per cent of the road network is paved. Despite an incredulous response from some industrialists ('Why not bring back black-and-white TVs and 78rpm records?' joked one), the competitively priced Fusca once again became a popular seller. More than 33,000 reborn Fuscas were produced up to the middle of 1995, and in 1994 the model was Brazil's twelfth best seller.

The 1990s' Fusca has undergone a number of modifications to comply with new safety and environmental regulations, and it is now fitted with a three-way catalytic converter, electronic ignition, a laminated windscreen, front disc brakes, a safety rear-view mirror and fire-resistant interior fabrics, and it meets Brazil's latest crash

Brazilian Fusca (alcohol-powered) (1996)

Engine

Type	Air-cooled ohv flat-four, twin-port cylinder heads, twin carburettors, catalytic converter
Capacity	1,584cc
Bore × stroke	86mm × 69mm
Compression ratio	11.0:1
Max. power	58bhp @ 4300rpm
Max. torque	86lb/ft @ 2800rpm

Transmission

Gearbox	Manual four-speed, synchro on all forward gears
Gear ratios	1st: 3.80
	2nd: 2.06
	3rd: 1.32
	4th: 0.88
	Reverse: 3.88
	Final drive: 3.88

Suspension

Front	Independent with transverse torsion bars and trailing arms; anti-roll bar
Rear	Independent with swing axles, transverse torsion bars and trailing arms

Brakes

Front disc, rear drum

Dimensions (in/mm)

Length	160/4,050
Width	61/1,540
Weight	1,820lb (825kg)

Performance

0–60mph	15sec
Top speed	87mph (139km/h)
Fuel consumption	27mpg (10.5l/100km)

Under the skin, the Fusca reveals a few changes. The engine is a 1600 unit, fitted with the unlikely combination of twin carburettors and a catalytic converter. An alcohol-powered version is also available.

test standards. Its 1,584cc engine still has twin carburettors, not fuel-injection, and once again there's the option of a version that uses alcohol instead of petrol.

MEXICAN BEETLES

Mexico's association with Volkswagen also go back a long way, to 1954 when the first VWs arrived in the country on the board the Dutch SS *Andyk*. Assembly of CDK

Beetles began soon after, but it took another ten years before Volkswagen de Mexico was set up. Only in 1967 did the first Beetle roll off the production lines at a plant built at Puebla, eighty miles (125km) from Mexico City.

The Beetle quickly became a success in Mexico, and production hit the half-million mark in 1975, by which time some 550 cars were leaving the production lines daily. In 1978, when production of the Beetle in Germany ended, the Mexican Beetle took

VW do Brasil have designed a new dashboard for their Fusca, with clock, speedo and fuel gauge.

its place, and was exported to European countries to meet the small but continuing demand from enthusiasts there.

The car they received was the 1200L, with a 34bhp engine. It was still based on the pre-1971 bodyshell, but featured such refinements as a fuel gauge, heated rear screen, inertia reel seat belts and adjustable head rests. Curiously, for some time these Mexican cars retained the Wolfsburg crest steering wheel badge.

Mexico produced the 20-millionth Beetle on 15 May 1981, and made 2,400 special edition Silver Bugs to commemorate the occasion. These were quickly snapped up, and their success set in motion the stream of special edition Beetles that Mexico made its speciality.

Despite these attempts to spice up the Beetle for export markets, the following years saw a gradual falling off in demand from Europe. New legislation restricted the number of countries in which Beetles could be sold. The Beetle failed to meet stringent Swiss exhaust noise laws passed in April 1983, and re-engineering it to meet them wasn't considered worthwhile. Finally, the last batch of Mexican Beetles to be sold officially in Europe reached Germany in August 1985.

Freed from the need to consider export markets, VW de Mexico was able to concentrate its efforts on adapting the Beetle more closely to local conditions. A 1,600cc version was introduced, with specially adapted carburettors to give better perfor-

Silver Bug was a Mexican special edition launched in 1981 to commemorate production of twenty million Beetles – the 2,400 Silver Bugs made quickly sold out.

mance in the rarefied atmosphere of Mexico City, 2,300 metres above sea level. Otherwise, the Mexican Beetle seemed to progress backwards for a while. It lost its fresh-air ventilation and rear heater outlets, rear seat belts were deleted and, rather short-sightedly, the dual-circuit brakes were replaced by the old single-circuit set-up. This was rectified in 1990 when dual-circuit brakes were reinstated. Tougher emissions regulations saw a catalytic converter arrive in 1991.

The next milestone in Mexican – and global – Beetle production came in 1992,

when the 21-millionth Beetle was completed on 23 June . This was celebrated by the launch of a 21 Millones special edition, so sought-after that all 6,000 of them sold out even before they were made.

Recent years have seen a surge in the technological development of the Mexican Beetle. In 1994 there were sweeping revisions to the flat-four, which gained fuel injection, maintenance-free hydraulic tappets and, at long last, a proper oil filter. Then in 1995 a 55amp alternator replaced the dynamo traditionally fitted to Mexican Beetles, and front disc brakes became stan-

The Beetle's last big celebration was in June 1992, when the 21 millionth Beetle came off the production line in Mexico. Roll on the next million!

dard. Changes for 1996 were mainly cosmetic, with the Beetle losing some of its brightwork in favour of a black paint finish.

The economic slump that hit Mexico in 1995 badly affected Beetle production, which actually ceased in the early summer for four months. Production at the start of the year was running at 450 cars per day, but at one stage it was down to barely 100.

It's still possible to buy and import a brand new Beetle, though regulations may well change in the future. Because the Mexican Sedan is more technologically advanced than the Brazilian Fusca, it's the one that Beetle enthusiasts in Europe usually go for. Often they pay a visit to Mexico and combine the transaction with a holiday. Because Beetles sell so cheaply in Mexico (around £5,000 in 1996), they don't end up being vastly expensive even after the various costs are taken into account.

Alternatively, several companies based in Germany import and sell Mexican Beetles. One of them, Beetles Revival, offers an extraordinary variety of optional extras, from a driver's air bag to heated front seats.

Mexican Beetle Sedan 1600i (1996)

Engine

Type	Air-cooled ohv flat-four, twin-port cylinder heads, hydraulic tappets, multi-point fuel injection, catalytic converter
Capacity	1,584cc
Bore × stroke	85.5mm × 69mm
Compression ratio	7.7:1
Max. power	44bhp @ 4,000rpm
Max. torque	70lb/ft @ 2,200rpm

Transmission

Gearbox	Manual four-speed, synchro on all forward gears
Gear ratios	1st: 3.80
	2nd: 2.06
	3rd: 1.32
	4th: 0.88
	Reverse: 3.78
	Final drive: 4.38

Suspension

Front	Independent with transverse torsion bars and trailing arms; anti-roll bar
Rear	Independent with swing axles, transverse torsion bars and trailing arms

Brakes   Front disc, rear drum

Dimensions (in/mm)

Length	160/4,060
Width	61/1,550
Weight	1,810lb (820kg)

Performance

0–60mph	20sec
Top speed	79mph (126km/h)
Fuel consumption	35mpg (8.1l/100km)

TOMORROW'S BEETLE?

Will the Beetle live forever? As long as it meets a local need, as it does in Mexico and Brazil, there seems little reason why production should end. However, even the Beetle, the most successful and prolific car of all time, can't defy the falling sands of time for ever. The Beetle is a car that has brought joy to millions of people, whether as a practical form of affordable motoring, a trendy style accessory, an off-beat racing vehicle, a pampered, cherished classic or just a much-loved family car. Will we ever see its like again?

Maybe. At the Detroit motor show in January 1994, a concept car was unveiled by VW R&D chief Ulrich Seiffert. Designed

Sedan 1600i.

Brochure for the Sedan 1600i shows that, despite many recent improvements, the Mexican Beetle still looks much the same as the car that was last made in Europe in 1978.

199

at VW's Californian studio, it was named Concept 1, and drew its inspiration directly from the Beetle.

The design team leader explained that, like Ferdinand Porsche and his Beetle, his team had approached the design of Concept 1 from an engineer's standpoint. Only what was absolutely necessary was included, with no superfluous styling curves or design tricks.

Like the Beetle, Concept 1's looks were entirely free of tension or aggression. It was shorter and wider than the Beetle, but still provided full four-seater capability. Safety was a prime feature in its design, with dual airbags, side impact bars, ABS and electro-luminescent lighting on the dash to reduce eyestrain.

The intention was that Concept 1 should be economical too, with the option of three different drivetrains: an electric/diesel hybrid (1,400cc diesel plus an 18kW electric motor); 1.9 turbo diesel ecomatic; or an 37kW electric motor with two-speed automatic transmission.

At the time Dr Seiffert commented:

The intention is to emphasize the typical qualities of a VW – its honest, reliable, timeless and youthful design.

We will never bring the Beetle back, but we would like to go back to our roots with an honest, reliable car. It will influence the design of our smaller product range, and in the future there will be more smaller cars on the road with these levels of comfort and safety.

Seiffert said categorically that the Concept 1 would never be turned into a production

Tomorrow's Beetle? Concept 1 is set to make the transition from concept car to production model, but will it be the people's car of the 21st Century, or just a plaything for the rich?

model. But the public thought differently.

Entranced by the Concept 1's good looks and elegant simplicity – to say nothing of its cheeky resemblance to the Beetle – the public deluged VW with requests to put it into production. In a rapid turnabout, in January 1995 VW announced that they had 'no option but to build the car before the end of the decade'.

After some deliberation about the name of the new model – at one stage 'Chico' looked the likeliest suggestion – Volkswagen bit the bullet and announced that when Concept 1 went into production it would indeed bear the same 'Beetle' nametag as its illustrious forebear. The path from concept to production is a tortuous one, and when we do finally get the chance to buy the new Beetle, it will be in a much-modified form to that original Detroit show car. Running prototypes suggest that the production car, based on the Golf floorpan, will be nine inches (240mm) longer than the original concept, and will

be capable of accepting any of the current Golf petrol or diesel engines, including the 174bhp VR6. Safety will be a high priority, with twin airbags, side-impact protection, anti-lock brakes and electronic traction control.

At the time of writing it isn't clear whether VW intends its new Beetle to be a cute fashion accessory for the well-heeled, or a serious budget car. It would be a shame if short-term considerations prompted VW to take the former course.

With massive markets for cheap transport poised to open up in India and China, what the world needs now every bit as much as it did in the 1930s when the original 'Volkswagen' people's car was conceived, is a small, cheap, rugged, practical car that is safe, clean and recyclable. If VW turns its new model into this vehicle, they might have on their hands a Beetle for the next century to rival the extraordinary success of the original in this one.

Index